D0625415

START AND RUN A

Sandwich and coffee shop

Visit our How To website at www.howto.co.uk

At www.howto.co.uk you can engage in conversation with our authors – all of whom have 'been there and done that' in their specialist fields. You can get access to special offers and additional content but most importantly you will be able to engage with, and become part of, a wide and growing community of people just like yourself.

At www.howto.co.uk you'll be able to talk and share tips with people who have similar interests and are facing similar challenges in their lives. People who, just like you, have the desire to change their lives for the better – be it through moving to a new country, starting a new business, growing their own vegetables, or writing a novel.

At www.howto.co.uk you'll find the support and encouragement you need to help make your aspirations a reality.

For more information on starting a sandwich and coffee shop visit www.startandrunasandwichandcoffeeshop.co.uk

How To Books strives to present authentic, inspiring, practical information in their books. Now, when you buy a title from **How To Books**, you get even more than just words on a page.

START AND RUN A

Sandwich and coffee shop

Jill Sutherland

howtobooks / **smallbusinessstart-ups**

Published by How To Books Ltd,
Spring Hill House, Spring Hill Road,
Begbroke, Oxford OX5 1RX, United Kingdom
Tel: (01865) 375794, Fax: (01865) 379162
info@howtobooks.co.uk
www.howtobooks.co.uk

British Library Cataloguing in Publication Data
A catalogue record for this book is available from the British Library

ISBN 978 1 84528 333 9

Produced for How To Books by Deer Park Productions, Tavistock
Typeset by Pantek Arts Ltd, Maidstone, Kent
Printed and bound in Great Britain by Bell & Bain Ltd, Glasgow

Every effort has been made to trace the copyright holders of material used in this book
but if any have inadvertently been overlooked the publishers will be pleased to make
the necessary arrangements at the first opportunity.

NOTE: The material contained in this book is set out in good faith for
general guidance and no liability can be accepted for loss or expense
incurred as a result of relying in particular circumstances on statements
made in the book. Laws and regulation are complex and liable to change,
and readers should check the current position with the relevant authorities
before making personal arrangements.

CONTENTS

ACKNOWLEDGEMENTS

I would first like to say a big thank you to How to Books, and to Nikki Read, for giving me the chance to write this book and to share my experiences with you.

Second, I would like to hijack this opportunity and cheekily say a huge thank you to the family, close friends and staff who helped us in the early days of our own café.

Christopher Jones, ex-owner of his own Cardiff sandwich bar, and the amazing mentor who held our hand through the first few weeks of opening. Keith Barber, the genius graphic designer who created amazing logos, posters and menus, and Richard Barrett who built our website. My dad Kevin, who created some of the most beautiful wooden shop counters. My mum Linda, Rhys and Bev, and Richard's sister Emma, who all helped out in the café in the early days, prepping food and waiting tables. Richard's mum Eileen, who bakes our delicious cakes. The band of merry leaflet droppers, including Katie, MLC, my brother Daniel, who obligingly donned our 'Taste' T-shirts and press-ganged anyone who'd listen into coming in for a coffee and a sandwich. And how can we fail to mention three particular members of staff who, through their hard work and dedication, have helped Taste to become the success it is . . . so thank you Lyn, Justyna and Paulina.

Finally, I would of course like to mention my wonderful husband Richard, without whose support, encouragement and belief none of this would have been possible . . .

INTRODUCTION

Dragons' Den, *The Apprentice*, *The Restaurant* . . . there are a multitude of programmes on television today promoting entrepreneurship and business acumen. It seems that everyone is looking for a way to escape the daily grind, and to capitalize on his or her big idea.

But why is this? Why are so many of us no longer happy to work nine to five for someone else? Lengthy commutes, longer working hours, decreasing pension reserves, diminishing family time; these are all reasons why many people, including myself and my husband Richard, decide to try to go it alone.

We, no doubt just as you are doing now, considered a number of possible business options before deciding to open our own sandwich bar. Having resolved to branch out on our own, we spent a summer holiday in Italy poring over masses of business start-up books, and brainstorming ideas. We were attracted by the (relatively) low start-up costs, the ability to create something unique and independent, and by the work–life balance a sandwich bar business would (eventually) offer us.

It is now almost three years since we opened Taste (UK) Ltd, and it has (thankfully) proved to be a reliable and secure source of income. After spending the first year or so with drastically tightened belts the business has now afforded us the opportunity to move house, get married and enjoy a life filled with variation and opportunity.

Aside from the masses of hard work, it has also been exciting, invigorating and immensely satisfying to create an idea, and then see it grow and bloom into a prosperous, award-winning business. But not only that; we are also greatly enjoying the opportunity we now have to share our experiences and to help other business owners to achieve their goals, and realize their dreams through the publication of this book, and through our mentoring business, Sutherland Communications (www.sutherlandcomms.com).

Through the coming chapters I hope to help you understand what to expect should you decide to take the leap, and how to make sure that your new business is the best that it can possibly be.

Taste (UK) Ltd, the business my husband Richard and I own, is an independent sandwich, salad and smoothie bar. However, we also often refer to it as a café, or simply a sandwich bar, and we also hear customers refer to it as a coffee bar or coffee shop. This book is written with this type of business in mind, but could also potentially help those readers planning to open a teashop with substantial relaxed seating areas, a delicatessen shop that also offers coffee and sandwiches, or a more traditional 'greasy spoon' type café.

Through this book I hope to support you during your opening year in business, from the initial idea to your first birthday celebrations. I hope that the experiences Richard and I have had in opening our own sandwich bar will help you to make the right decisions for your own, and that you achieve the business success and change in lifestyle you are aiming for.

HOW TO USE THIS BOOK

I've written this book for people who are already employed, but who are hoping to resign that employment and begin their own sandwich bar business.

I have structured the chapters in the order Richard and I carried out the work prior to opening our own sandwich bar. With this in mind we hope you'll find the book useful in three ways. First, by reading it cover to cover you'll gain an honest insight into what you can expect if you decide to go it alone. Second, once you've decided to take the leap, by working through the book chapter by chapter you'll give a defined structure to the opening of your new business. And third, once you've opened we hope you'll also find the book to be a quick and easy flick-through manual, providing hands-on advice for your own particular sandwich bar situation.

Within each chapter you'll find the following:

☐ **At a Glance** – A rapid glimpse of what is contained in the chapter.

☐ **Top Tips** – Our own experiences will provide you with some hints, tips and must dos and don'ts.

☐ **Alarm Bells** – These flash up throughout the book; ignore them at your peril!

☐ **Café Culture** – Real-life stories from the creation of and day-to-day running of our own sandwich bar Taste will hopefully give you an insight into what to *really* expect.

1
BEFORE YOU TAKE THE PLUNGE!

AT A GLANCE

In this chapter we'll cover:

☐ The sandwich and coffee bar marketplace – whether it's growing, and if there's room in it for you.

☐ Your suitability, and the personality traits and skills you'll need to succeed.

☐ A day in the life of a sandwich bar owner – what to expect, and what to prepare yourself for.

The marketplace – not a bed of roses

The UK has undergone a massive transformation in terms of high street day-time eateries. Think back ten years or so and on most medium-sized high streets you would have found a pub, a fish and chip shop, a McDonald's and a local bakery.

Take a stroll down your local high street now and things could not look more different. Shop after shop has been taken over by food retailers. Subway, O'Brien's, Gregg's, Pret A Manger, Eat, Costa, Starbucks, Caffè Nero . . . not to mention the various restaurants, supermarkets and garages that offer day-time lunch options. Think of what you fancy to eat or drink and you'll be bamboozled by a choice of wraps, bagels, paninis, sushi, smoothies, pasties, salads, sandwiches, subs, burgers, wheat grass shots and mocha chocca latte cappuccinos!

The UK has readily embraced the 'café society', and a sandwich bar or coffee shop is often viewed as a leisure experience rather than simply a place to eat and drink. Many people are also moving away from the pub culture, and sandwich bars are seen as an alternative place to meet and catch up. With this in mind, your sandwich bar's customers will likely fall into these categories.

☐ Women, who prefer the sandwich bar, coffee shop environment to that of a pub. They feel comfortable sitting alone in the non-threatening environment.

□ Young and affluent professionals, who eat out far more than any other sector of society.

□ Office workers, who buy their daily breakfast, lunch or perhaps both.

□ Older customers, who like high-quality, personal service. This group has the potential to drastically improve your off-peak sales.

□ Shoppers, who will make up a large percentage of a sandwich bar's 'eat in' revenue.

So, before you decide whether there's room for you, and your new café, you need to take a long, hard and very honest look at the industry. Make sure you weigh up the positives . . . and don't ignore the negatives.

On the positive side:

□ The explosion in choice has helped to increase the market's size, and more and more people now opt to buy their breakfast and lunch on the go, rather than preparing it themselves at home.

□ This is also driven by consumers' busier lives; in the UK we have the longest commuting times and the longest working hours in Europe.

□ Consumers are becoming increasingly engaged with the food they eat, and want to know exactly what they are buying and eating. Words like traceability, sustainability, organic, locally produced, handmade, home-made, are all on the agenda. Good news for the owner-run café.

□ Consumers are prepared to pay more for a quality product. TNS data shows that the average sandwich in the UK now costs £1.85, an all-time high.

□ Consumers are enjoying a renaissance of Britishness, with traditional British foods and cuisine enjoying a resurgence in popularity.

On the negative side, however:

□ The explosion in daytime eateries has made the marketplace more and more competitive. This means that as an independent café you'll have to be ingenious and flawless in order to succeed.

□ High street rents have rocketed, as have business rates and service charges.

□ Food prices have risen, and will continue to rise in the future.

☐ Staff costs can be expensive, with regulations such as the minimum wage, and mandatory holiday and sick pay for casual part-time staff.

☐ New guidelines for detailed food labelling for packed sandwiches have been introduced, and the industry is under pressure from the government to meet new health guidelines, for example, in relation to salt levels in foods.

Added to all this you'll also be aware that the economy is not as buoyant as it was. At the time of writing, newspapers are full of headlines warning of an economic recession, a house market crash and general financial slowdown.

Will we, won't we? It's incredibly hard to know for sure whether the UK will slide into economic depression. What I do know is that business in my café is still growing year on year. However, I also know that for a new sandwich bar just starting out the uphill struggle of becoming established will be that bit steeper in the current economic climate.

In fact, accountancy firm Deloitte have recently stated that in their view it has never been more difficult to build a successful, sustainable and socially responsible food and beverage business in the UK. Why? Well, as their report *Food and Beverage 2012 – a taste of things to come* highlights, higher commodity prices have become the norm rather than a temporary peak, and the high cost of food produce represents a permanent step change, not a blip.

Beginning in 2005, and for the first time since the 1970s, food prices have been increasing substantially. As a result, since 2000 the price of wheat has tripled. In 2007 alone, wheat prices rose 52%. For food retailers this means that they have to be as competitive as they can be; they need to really differentiate their products, and have strong brands, innovative products or services and a superior customer experience.

So, starting your own sandwich bar is not going to be easy, and once it's up and running you'll never be able to take your foot off the gas. Are you prepared for that? My advice is, ask yourself some tough questions, do masses of research, and take the leap only when you're absolutely certain.

If you are prepared to be flexible, work harder than you've ever worked before, and have a good feel for food, then you have every chance of making a success of your business, earning a reasonable income, and securing an asset for your future along the way.

Your suitability – will it be right for you?

Setting up your own business, especially a food retail business, is all-consuming. If you're going to succeed and be happy you'll need to assess whether you're suitable, and whether your skills and personality are up to the job.

CAN YOU MULTI-TASK?

You'll be a managing director, a financial director, an operations director, a human resources manager, a food development technician and a marketing consultant all rolled into one. Added to that you'll be a shop assistant, a waiter and a general dogsbody, and all these jobs muddled into any given hour spent running your business.

ARE YOU RESILIENT?

You'll face many situations that demand an ability to bounce back, from the birth of your business right through to the day-to-day running of an established one.

Café Culture

Back in 2006, when we were looking for our first café premises, we hit upon numerous seemingly insurmountable obstacles. Many retail landlords would not consider us for their empty shop units because we were a new business with no trading history. When we did find a unit, and begin negotiations, we discovered the landlord wanted a six-month rent deposit, an impossible amount for a new business to hand over. The day before opening, our fridge and freezer equipment still had not arrived, despite promises to the contrary from the supplier. In those early months each day threw up another issue to be dealt with and sorted out.

Today we have to remain as resilient as we were then. Yes, with an established business there are fewer surprises, but with the pressures of any average day it would be easy to become disheartened. It's certainly a skill to be able to deal adeptly with an obnoxious, rude or even aggressive customer, and then continue to serve the queue, unperturbed and unfazed.

Being honest, I have not always found it easy, and even today I'll occasionally become bothered when customers throw money on the counter, or fail to say please or thank you. But on the whole I have learnt to take a deep breath, smile and move on to the next, usually polite, customer. This skill is imperative, or you'll end up going round the twist!

ARE YOU A GOOD HOST?

Do you regularly entertain? When you do, do you consider all of your guests' needs, put special thought into drinks to be served, how the table will be laid, what dessert will compliment the main meal? Or do you like a party to be thrown together, last minute, organized by somebody else?

The fact is that owning your own café is very much like playing the host every day. You need to welcome your customers, make them feel at home, consider their every need, surprise them, impress them, entertain them. In fact, building a relationship with your customers is no different from building a relationship with a new friend.

In my experience, to succeed, hospitality has to come naturally to you. If it does not then you'll find it very difficult to develop the high levels of customer service demanded by today's customer. Remember, they have lots of choice, and if they don't feel special and cared for in your café, then they'll go to someone else's.

DO YOU LOVE FOOD?

Are you interested in understanding the difference between lettuce flavours – lollo rosso vs iceberg, cos vs rocket? Would you see the point in spending an hour tasting various chutneys to ensure you choose a perfect match for the mature Cheddar you serve with your ploughman's? Do you know the difference between low GI and high GI – do you care?

Café Culture

An elderly couple came into our café, and sat at a table in the window. They ordered tea and toast and sat back down. Just as my staff member was taking the tea to them, I noticed their table had been moved, and was now wobbling on the uneven surface. I quickly nipped over, asked the staff member to wait, and readjusted the feet on the table so it no longer wobbled. A tiny gesture, but it was one that they greatly appreciated. It showed that we were taking notice of our customers, and cared about their happiness and enjoyment. They may have been spending only a small amount of money that morning, but they left feeling like they were the most important customers in the shop, and they came back the next week, with friends, for lunch!

The fact is that most people who buy a freshly made sandwich or salad at lunchtime, rather than a pre-packed one, value the expertise of the person making it. To please your customers, and to compete against the multitude of other lunchtime choices, you need to be passionate, innovative and knowledgeable.

IS IT ALL ABOUT THE MONEY?

Sounds like a negative, right? Wrong! The end goal of all businesses is to make money. Yes, your day-to-day focus should be on fantastic food, amazing customer service, happy staff . . . but the reason for all your hard work, the very purpose of your business, is to make you money. So you should never, ever forget that yes, it is all about the money.

It's all too easy at the beginning to have a romantic ideal of a happy café, smiling customers, huge portions, free coffee top-ups. Of course you want happy customers, but you also want a happy bank account. To succeed in business the two must go hand in hand. The key is to find the balance, and you'll achieve that by being efficient, monitoring portion control and keeping a close eye on the bottom line.

Café Culture

We were busy from day one, with many customers ordering sandwiches, salads and jacket potatoes for lunch. However, five months after opening we began to notice that although the daily takings were good, the profit margin, after bills had been paid, was lower than we'd like. In short, we were working really hard to serve lots of customers, but not making quite enough at the end of the day to make it worthwhile. The answer was portion control. We spent time with staff retraining them on the number of spoonfuls of fillings to use in sandwiches, salads, etc. Within a week we could see a visible difference to the bottom line, and the profits began to reach the healthy 65% figure we always aim for.

I did struggle in the beginning to really grasp the importance of tight financial management. Thankfully my husband Richard had experience in this area and so we focused on it from day one. If like me this is not your strength area, I would recommend you learn as much as you can as quickly as you can through bookkeeping and accountancy courses, or enlist the help of a friend who can work with you. Lose track of the bottom line and your business could flounder before it's even begun. Because this area is so important to the success of your business we cover it in depth in Chapter 4.

A day in the life

If you've never worked in food retail before, as we hadn't, then it is virtually impossible to truly imagine what to expect. So, I'll give you an example of what an average day might look like:

☐ **6.45am. Arrive at your café and begin work.** Depending on the size and scale of your café you'll be either on your own or with just a staff member or two. Either way, before you open you'll be turning on and checking machinery, conducting fridge temperature checks, signing off deliveries such as bread, meats, cheeses, milk and salad stuffs. Setting out tables, unstacking chairs, setting up work stations with butter, knives and greaseproof paper. Restocking supplies of cups, spoons, sugar, salt and pepper sachets, etc.

☐ **7.30am. Open to the public.** Breakfast is hectic. Not only are you (hopefully) serving a busy queue of hungry office workers tempted by your delicious toast and coffee, you're also preparing your café for the day. In a sandwich bar like ours this means preparation of all of our own sandwich fillings; it also means the preparation of home-made coleslaw and potato salad, and washing and slicing the salad stuffs such as lettuce, cucumber, tomato and onion. Even if you decide to buy in your sandwich fillings and mixes, this time of the day is going to be frenetic, with so much to prepare and customers to serve. You'd better be a morning person!

☐ **9.30am. Mid-morning.** The breakfast rush has died down, and the preparation of fillings and salad stuffs is coming to an end. Now you need to turn your attention to preparing the sandwich platters you have to deliver to local offices for meetings at lunchtime. You also need to ensure that the refrigerated serve-over counters are stocked and looking beautiful. On top of this you need to listen out for the telephone and monitor email for customer orders. And if that's not enough, you need to continue to serve your mid-morning customers, popping in for coffee and a slice of cake. Make sure you've a smile and a kind word for everyone.

☐ **11am. Pre-lunch.** This is usually the quietest time of day, so you'll be grabbing a bite to eat, checking your email, opening the post, approving holiday requests, updating timesheets, fixing a wobbly chair leg, posting supplier cheques, nipping to the bank to pay in cash or collect bags of coin change.

☐ **12 noon. Lunch.** You will, I hope, be stressed and busy. But, importantly, under control, because of all the time spent preparing during the morning.

You should expect an extremely noisy environment: the coffee machine and perhaps a smoothie blender competing with customers placing orders, staff passing requests, those seated laughing and chatting. You'll have to be on the ball at all times, instructing staff, serving customers, watching for signs of any potential problems that may upset things. If your café is popular you won't come up for air until around 2.30pm. No break, no toilet stop, no time to think – can you handle it?

□ **2.30pm onwards. Clean down.** After a day spent on your feet you now need to maintain the momentum and ensure that the clean down of the café is carried out thoroughly, while still serving the steady trickle of late lunch customers and afternoon coffee breaks. You'll be emptying and cleaning the serve-over counters, replacing and restocking serving dishes of food, wiping tables, sweeping and mopping floors, washing through the coffee machine, cleaning and sanitizing microwaves, ovens, contact grills, cupboard doors and handles of fridges. You'll also be getting ready to start all over again the next day by writing out lists of foods that need to be prepared the following morning, putting in stock orders for deliveries, and re-stocking drinks fridges and snack shelves.

□ **4pm. Close.** Your café may be closed to customers, but you can expect to put in another couple of hours, catching up with admin work, thinking about next week's sandwich specials, scheduling in your staff appraisals, chasing payment from business customers who order platters. At the end of your 11-hour day you can have dinner at home and think about how to grow your business even more!

Add into the mix unhappy customers, deliveries that don't turn up, equipment that breaks down, staff who are sick, an unannounced environmental health officer (EHO) visit, and you'll probably begin to see just how important it is to be organized and unflappable, a natural communicator, excellent at delegating, and most of all, how important it'll be that you genuinely enjoy working in your sandwich bar.

 Perhaps consider signing up to a site such as www.925dream.co.uk, through which you can gain access to work experience packages designed to give you a real feel for running your own café. Look out for Taste under the catering section!

2
PLANNING YOUR BUSINESS

AT A GLANCE

In this chapter we'll cover:

☐ Do your research
  – Getting started, creating 'sandwich bar HQ'.
  – The importance of research and key research tactics to employ.

☐ Your big idea and turning it into reality
  – What is it exactly?

☐ Write your business plan
  – What you should include and how to write it.
  – What start-up costs you can expect.
  – Cash flow forecasting.

☐ Setting up your business
  – Sole trader or limited company?
  – Finding the right accountant and solicitor.
  – Dealing with Companies House.

☐ When and how to take the leap
  – Understanding when and how to leave your current employment.

☐ Finding your premises
  – Creating the brief, what to consider.
  – Working with agents – getting agents to work for you!
  – Doing the deal (and making sure it's a good one).
  – Understanding licences (A1, A2, A3).

☐ Creating your brand identity
  – Finding the right name
  – Deciding on your sandwich bar's 'identity'.

Do your research

You are no longer a civilian! Now, every waking moment of your day should be spent testing, trying, asking, examining, learning and researching. The aim of the next few months is to put your burgeoning idea under the microscope, to consider it alongside actual businesses, and to become an expert in the marketplace you hope to join. All of this hard work is designed to help you to formulate as plausible a plan as possible for your own business.

STAY SANE WHILE RESEARCHING!

With so much to research it's very easy to get sidetracked and lose sight of your objectives. These top tips should help you find a sense of structure, and enable you to hold on to your sanity!

- **Set up an office** – No matter how cluttered or full your home is, it's vital that you set aside a space to be your sandwich bar HQ. It doesn't matter whether this is a spare bedroom or one half of the kitchen table. The important thing is to designate space, and have an organized work area, with a computer, internet access and a phone.
- **Create a scrapbook** – We suggest keeping any menus, newspaper clippings and magazine articles that may be relevant to your new sandwich bar. Perhaps also have a 'mood board' and tack up the various pictures, words or menus that describe the kind of café you want to create. Have this somewhere prominent; it'll help keep you focused and motivated.
- **Use to do lists** – My friends giggle at my constant list-making, but when you've millions of tasks to juggle it is the only sensible way to keep organized.
- **Be tidy** – At the end of each working day tidy away your work so that your desk is fresh and ready for tomorrow. Use this time to filter what you've gathered and dispose of any material that's no longer useful.

By the end of the next few months you'll know the industry you're about to join, and understand the marketplace your sandwich bar will operate in. You'll have a good knowledge of the possible suppliers you'd use, which equipment you'd install, and how much produce and equipment will cost you. You'll appreciate the business costs likely to be associated with staffing, leasing premises, energy supply and business rates. In short, you'll have given your idea a reality check.

To make sure that your research is thorough I suggest that you work through the tactics outlined below.

TRY OUT THE COMPETITION

You'd better join a gym, as you'll be trying out as many sandwiches, paninis, ciabattas, cakes, wraps, bagels and jacket potatoes as you can, from as many different types of outlet as you can manage. Don't just visit the kind of places you already frequent, try places you don't like the look of, and visit cafés that sell the kinds of food you don't usually eat. Don't forget to visit the big chains too – they're not big chains by chance. They're obviously good at what they do, and there's no harm in copying an idea or two for your own business.

Make notes on presentation, portion size, quality of produce; check the packaging and labelling for practicality and user-friendliness. Take note of the style of the café – the way it's decorated, the uniform of the staff, whether the ordering and preparation system is organized and efficient. What do you like, what don't you like, what works, what does not?

Get into character as a spy! Try and spot which coffee machines, fridges, blenders, etc. various cafés are using. Note down the names, and model numbers. Make a note of which drinks, crisps and snack brands are being sold.

Always have your embryonic idea in the back of your mind, and begin to build a draft plan of what foods you'll serve, how your café will look, how your food will be served.

Also make notes of things to avoid, and why. Collect as many menus as possible, and pick up any other marketing material cafés have on display, such as customer loyalty cards, adverts for special offers, seasonal food leaflets. These will all come in handy when you go on to design your own brand identity (see later in this chapter) and marketing plan (Chapter 4).

Café Culture

In the first months of our idea development Richard and I visited hundreds of sandwich bars, cafés, coffee shops and tearooms. We collected filing cabinet loads of menus, and filled notebook after notebook with observations from the places we visited. Every week we'd organize our research, pinpointing the positives that we wanted to build into our own plan, and flagging up the negatives that we knew we wanted to avoid. Each week our idea became clearer and clearer in our heads; the food we'd serve, the systems we'd use, and the way our staff would be dressed.

At this stage of our planning and research we became a subscriber to *Sandwich and Snack News*, the trade magazine for the industry. We found it to be a very informative read, and it made us aware of many issues that could affect our developing business. To learn more call 01291 628103 or visit www.sandwich.org.uk.

MONITOR PRICES

While on your reconnaissance missions remember to keep a close eye on pricing, as this is one of the most important things to get right when running a sandwich bar. Ironically it's also one of the hardest, especially when you're new to the business.

You certainly should not simply 'copy' the prices that a similar sandwich bar charges on its menu, but you should take note of the range of prices charged by varying competitors for a similar product. When you come to develop your own pricing structure (Chapter 3) this research, and the menus you've collected will be invaluable.

Alarm Bell

You're excited! You can't wait to get started! You dream about the day you open the doors to your first customer. STOP. It's important that you ignore the temptation to rush ahead.

In our first two years of trading we saw many cafés and sandwich bars open, and then close. One of the main reasons for these businesses not succeeding, as we had, was that the owners had clearly not spent enough time researching and understanding the local market, customers and location.

VISIT TRADE SHOWS

In the months before opening, while you are developing your idea and business plan, sourcing suppliers and developing your menu, it's vital to visit as many trade shows as possible. Some you'll find incredibly useful, some will provide you with only a few pieces of new information. The important thing is that you're submerging yourself in the industry, and enabling yourself to gather as much information as possible.

Caffe Culture – Olympia, May

We found this show to be incredibly useful. Its main focus is on the coffee side, but it has a broad mix of exhibitors including speciality bread producers, deli suppliers and packaging firms. It also had a number of useful workshops covering topics such as 'starting up a coffee shop business', 'coffee machine maintenance', and 'new flavours in coffee'. Visit www.caffeculture.com.

International Food Expo (IFE) – Excel, March

IFE was one of the first trade shows we visited. It's huge; its exhibitors take up almost the entire Excel exhibition space. It's very easy to get sidetracked and loose focus if you're not extremely organized about what you want to achieve from the day. As a global food and drink event it usually splits its food and drink exhibitors into national pavilions, so if you know you're not likely to sell Mexican food then you should avoid spending time in that area. We found it provided an excellent opportunity to source products and suppliers, and get inspiration. It too had workshops and seminars, tackling current trends such as sustainability, provenance and health issues, plus live cooking demonstrations and practical tips on flavours and menu creation. Visit www.ife.co.uk.

The Taste Experience – Olympia, November

This event is organized by the British Sandwich Association. It's much smaller than the two listed above, but is certainly worth attending. If you've visited IFE you probably won't find any new exhibitors in attendance; however, the seminars are particularly useful and often the speakers are from chains such as Pret A Manger and government organizations such as the Food Standards Agency. Visit www.sandwich.org.uk.

Lunch! – Billingsgate, September

This is a new trade show, but stands to be a very useful one. It's billed as a contemporary show for the new and changing 'food to go' market. It'll provide you with an opportunity to source new products, find out about the latest 'food to go' market trends and network with other industry professionals. It should also boast lots of new up and coming food suppliers, who have developed interesting products based on consumers' current likes and dislikes. Visit www.lunchshow.co.uk.

As well as these broad industry-wide exhibitions there are also many more specific trade shows that could benefit your research. This includes regional food fairs showcasing regional smaller producers, organic food festivals – the biggest of which is held in Harrogate in November – and packaging and equipment shows such as Pro2Pak, held in March at Excel.

The ideal time to begin attending exhibitions such as these is once you've formed a solid image of what your café will be like, and the kind of food and service you want to provide. If you attend with this approach then you'll be armed with a filter for the barrage of information that you're faced with, and be able to gather only what is relevant to your idea. You should leave with bagloads of leaflets and flyers from various suppliers who could provide you with the food, drink and equipment that you'll need for your shop. Be sure to make notes on these flyers, outlining whether you felt the contact was a positive one, and any potential issues that occured to you. Once you get back home it's very difficult to remember every business and every contact you made!

GET IN TOUCH WITH SUPPLIERS

Your idea does not have to be concrete for you to begin talking to suppliers. At this stage you'll have masses of information collected at trade shows, and names of equipment manufacturers jotted down from your reconnaissance visits to other cafés. Start getting in touch, explain your situation, and give them an outline of the kind of café you'll be opening, and the kind of foods you'd like to serve. Ask them to send brochures, and recommend items to you, giving price breakdowns, etc.

In our experience suppliers and manufacturers are most happy to help you at this stage, before the deal is sealed, so to speak. Make the most of this. Ask for their advice: what do their other small independent café customers sell, use, benefit from buying? Visit coffee suppliers. Try out their training suite and get used to different types of coffee machines. Don't be afraid to ask, because most of the time they'll be happy to accommodate your request if they think you'll be a new customer.

GET SOME WORK EXPERIENCE

If, like us, you've never worked in food retail before, then I'd highly recommend getting some work experience in a similar café or sandwich bar. If you have a location in mind for your business, then perhaps consider looking a little further afield for your work experience; the owner may not take kindly to helping a would-be competitor learn the ropes.

Café Culture

We were lucky enough to make contact with a café owner by chance, through a fridge auction on ebay. The café was a deli-catessen-based business, which offered eat-in and takeaway coffee and sandwiches as an additional service. I spent two valuable days working there (for free of course!), helping in the kitchen, serving customers at lunchtime, waiting tables, making sandwiches to order. It gave me a good insight into the processes that need to be in place, and the speed at which you have to be able to serve at lunchtime. I came away with masses of ideas to ensure the smooth running of my own café.

SIGN UP WITH BUSINESS PROPERTY AGENTS

At this early stage it's important to begin painting a picture of the possible financial costs associated with leasing or buying premises for your business.

You should begin by getting in touch with local agents and registering your interest. Take a walk down a few of your local city, town, village high streets and jot down the contact details from their 'for rent' boards. Your requirements will depend on the type of sandwich bar or café you wish to open, but a reasonable initial brief, designed to provide as broad a picture as possible, would look something like this.

Retail unit required for sandwich bar / coffee shop. A1 or A3 usage licence. 500–2000 sq ft. On or near high street, or in prominent location with high footfall (i.e. near office district / university / trading estate, etc). Would consider new lease and re-assignment.

Don't feel pressured to give too much information away at this stage; the agent does not need to know the ins and outs of your idea. Explain that you are at the initial research stage of your project, and are hoping to gain an understanding of what retail premises are available for what rent/price in the local area.

MAKE THE MOST OF THE WEB

It's not easy to visit every kind of sandwich and coffee bar currently operating in the UK, but that's no excuse for not understanding them, what they are about, and what makes them successful. Google names like Eat, Pret A Manger, Costa, Caffé Nero, Benugo, Bagel Nash, Starbucks and O'Brien's and you'll be fascinated with the masses of information you can gather from corporate websites. It's not just the big chains that have websites either. Up and coming London-based independents such as Grazing, Fuzzy's Grub and Energy Box have their own websites, and regional chains such as Birmingham's Philpotts and Bristol's Chandos Deli may prove useful too. Search Yell.com for your own local sandwich bars, and find links to their websites from the directory.

When doing internet searches, if you use quotation marks to define your search, the results will be far more focused (something I only recently found out). For example, try typing 'sandwich bars' into Google's engine, instead of simply sandwich bars.

Also useful are information-sharing sites, such as www.freepint.com. Membership is free, and you'll join an online business community happy to share statistics, facts and reports with you.

VISIT A BUSINESS LIBRARY

Your local business library will be an excellent source for newspapers, trade magazines, reports and directories. If you've time, and money, my advice would be to plan a day trip to London's City Business Library, and study the wide and varied choice of Mintel and Frost and Sullivan market research reports. To make your day really worthwhile, use the time in London to visit the café hot spots to try out some exciting eateries. Try Covent Garden, Soho, Bank and Canary Wharf. You'll be amazed at the variety of different takes on the traditional sandwich bar, and will gain some really useful ideas for your own place.

Your big idea and turning it into reality

You've spent time researching the marketplace; you've visited a multitude of sandwich bars in your geographical area and you are well versed on what is currently on offer. You've read as much as you can on the topic of consumer trends, and have a good understanding of what today's food buyers are looking for from their local sandwich and coffee bar. You know roughly where you'd like your business to be based, and have an excellent understanding of what the competition will be on your chosen high street. You've established ballpark costings for equipment and food produce.

In our experience there are four major areas that you need to research and understand before you can be sure that your sandwich bar idea has potential. We suggest you stick to these areas, or you could become bogged down and muddled.

- **The market** – There are two important areas: the industry, and your local area. First, you need to understand the industry you'll be entering, and how your business will fit into it. How big is the sandwich and coffee bar market? What are the past, present and future trends in food and drink sales? What issues are affecting other sandwich and coffee bar owners? Second, what is the size of your local market? If you're planning on locating in a shopping centre, what is the footfall of customers per day? How many other sandwich bars and cafés are there? What percentage of the footfall could you realistically expect to serve through your café?

- **Customers** – Who are your customers? Are they health conscious or money conscious? Are they city workers in a hurry, or young mums with time to chat? You should work out the average customer's buying habits, likes and dislikes. What price would they be willing to pay, what kind of experience will they want? Using this picture of your average customer, also consider whether there is something new, and unique, that your café can offer them, something that is missing from other cafés in the area.

- **Competition** – You simply must understand your opponents. Which cafés will you be competing against, and what are their strengths and weaknesses? How long have they been established – are they successful? How does your business differ from theirs? What food and drink do they specialize in? What price do they sell it at?

> • **Suppliers** – You need to have a good basic understanding of how much produce and equipment will cost. How much is a coffee machine, and can you lease rather than buy? How much will bread cost, and the fillings? Can you charge your target customer enough in order to cover the costs and make money?

So, based on all this knowledge, what business do you want to create? To help hone your burgeoning idea you need to undertake a three-step exercise.

STEP 1 – PICTURE YOUR CAFÉ

Take a look at your scrapbook and mood board. Create a picture of exactly the café you want to own. This is all about *you* and what makes you excited.

☐ When you close your eyes, do you imagine yourself owning a small, bustling sandwich bar, designed for workers on the go? Perhaps you can see a lounge-style tearoom for university students or young mums to visit during the day? Or even a delicatessen brimming with cold meats and cheeses, and offering sandwiches as well.

☐ What kind of food are you passionate about? Is it home-cooked food? Do you harbour ambitions to make and sell your own chutneys, soups, pies? Or are you a lover of traditional fare, breakfast baps and foot-long subs? Perhaps you're knowledgeable about low GI foods, and have an interest in food intolerance, and health?

☐ Of all the cafés and sandwich bars you've visited, which are the ones that *you* most liked? Did you like the traditional, made-to-order sandwich counter approach, or were you impressed by sandwich bars that chose to make up the sandwiches in the morning, to be sold at lunchtime?

☐ Write down a 'brain dump' of all the words that spring to mind when you think about your 'perfect' café – e.g. small, friendly, local, fresh, home-made, canteen, large, low budget . . .

STEP 2 – PICTURE THE LOCATION

Think about the geographic area you intend to open your business in, and decide what is required from a new sandwich bar. Ask yourself questions such as:

☐ What kind of people live and work in this area? Are they highly paid office workers and affluent families, or are they a mix of more price-conscious consumers?

☐ What competitor sandwich bars already exist in this area? Do the local high streets have a Gregg's? An M&S? Do any other independent sandwich bars already exist? Have you come across Costa and Starbucks? What about Subway?

☐ What have you identified as 'missing'? Is there a lack of traditional sandwich bars offering simple made-to-order sandwiches? Have you spotted a need for a higher-quality café serving innovative new fillings and breads? Do you believe that potential customers in this area would welcome a café specialising in wraps and smoothies?

☐ Write down a 'brain dump' of the words that spring to mind when you think about the geographic area you intend to open your business in – e.g. well off, on a budget, students, highly paid, young, OAP, busy workers . . .

STEP 3 – PUT THE TWO TOGETHER

Meld the two pictures. The key to owning a successful sandwich bar is to be passionate and have a personal interest in your business, while at the same time offering the area's consumers what they want. There's absolutely no point in opening a sandwich bar that you and your friends like if it is offering the exact opposite of what the majority of people in the area like to eat.

Café Culture

We love healthy food, and like a simple functional environment. However, we also know that a large percentage of people living and working in the area where our café is based have simpler tastes, and like a cosy spot to enjoy a mug of tea. For this reason we curbed our desire to make Taste a showcase for extreme healthy modern living. We knew this kind of café would alienate too many people. Instead we created a hybrid, taking the best of the health food café, and adding back in some home comforts and traditional sandwich bar foods.

The good news is that your idea does not have to be earth-shattering or ground-breaking, or even totally unique or original. The world of sandwich bars is full of successes that are simply a modification on the basic theme.

Write your business plan

Now that you've come to the end of your initial research stage, and have developed a clear vision of what you want your sandwich bar to be like, you will begin to ask yourself how you can turn your idea into a real business. The first and most important step is to write a business plan. It does not matter whether you intend to invest tens of thousands in an all-singing, all-dancing café eatery, or a few thousand pounds into a sandwich kiosk, the importance of developing a business plan should not be underestimated.

The reason why writing a business plan is so important is that at the moment your idea (great as it may be) is simply that – an idea. To turn it into a profitable business you need to focus on planning, on processes and on systems. You'll need to provide a business plan for any investors, including the bank. In addition, landlords may ask to see your business plan before approving you as a new tenant.

It might sound scary, and technical and intimidating, but don't worry. Your business plan is simply a list of the objectives you want to achieve, the time frame you'll achieve them in, and an overview of the budget along the way.

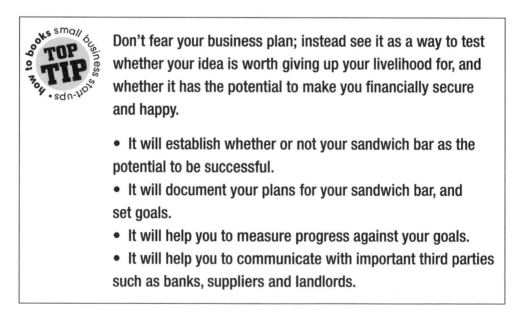

Don't fear your business plan; instead see it as a way to test whether your idea is worth giving up your livelihood for, and whether it has the potential to make you financially secure and happy.

- It will establish whether or not your sandwich bar as the potential to be successful.
- It will document your plans for your sandwich bar, and set goals.
- It will help you to measure progress against your goals.
- It will help you to communicate with important third parties such as banks, suppliers and landlords.

WHAT YOUR BUSINESS PLAN SHOULD INCLUDE

Every business plan is different. Here I have outlined the format we followed, in order to get you started.

☐ **About you** – Who you are, your experience, your skills, especially as this relates to your planned business.

☐ **Your sandwich bar idea** – What will your sandwich bar be like, what will it serve, will the food be made to order or made in advance, what will make it different, special?

☐ **Your customers** – Who your customers will be, what they will like, dislike, where they currently buy their lunch, how many potential customers exist in your locality.

☐ **Consumer demand** – Why your customers will like your sandwich bar, and buy your food.

☐ **Price point** – What your food will cost, giving evidence that your customers will pay this price for your food.

☐ **Sales** – How much you believe your customers will spend per visit, how often you believe they will visit you each day, each week?

☐ **Costs** – How much it will cost you to make each sandwich, jacket potato, etc.

☐ **The initial investment** – How much it will cost you to open your sandwich bar, decorate the café, buy staff uniforms, etc.

☐ **My sandwich bar will be a success because** – Explain why you believe your business has the potential to be a success and make money.

☐ **Summary** – Bullet list of the key points of your plan: short and concise, can be understood in a flash.

WHAT START-UP COSTS YOU CAN EXPECT

We found that the start-up costs of a sandwich bar were significantly lower than other retail businesses – for example, there is not a requirement to spend tens of thousands on expensive stock to fill the shop. However, substantial capital may be required. Suitable premises need to be leased, and a central location will be expensive. The appearance of the shop will also be vital, so much of the budget needs to be allocated to fixtures and fittings. The scale of your business will obviously dictate the true start-up costs, but, if you're coming from a non-catering background as we did, how on earth will you estimate such amounts? Is £3K a good price for a traditional espresso machine, or are you being ripped off?

The answer, as always, is lots of research. To start you on the right track, the following is a breakdown of some of the costs you should expect. More detailed advice on which equipment to choose for your sandwich bar can be found in Chapter 3.

☐ **Serve-over fridge counter** – Counters range in size from a basic 1 metre in length, to purpose-built extended units. Depending on size, serve-over chilled counters range from £1,000 for smaller units to upwards to tens of thousands of pounds for purpose-built ones. For the purposes of most sandwich shops a new, but basic, model will suffice, with an average cost point being around £1,500 per counter.

☐ **Coffee machine** – Coffee machines range in type and size. Some are automatic and make the coffee at the push of a button, while others are manual and require you to tamp the coffee and steam the milk. The machine that's right for your business depends on how big a part coffee will play in everyday sales. Always avoid second-hand machines (they're complicated, and it's difficult to assess wear and tear) and budget between £3,000 and £4,000 for a new machine.

☐ **Kitchen fridges and freezers** – Otherwise known as 'uprights'. You will certainly require some catering-grade fridges and freezers in your sandwich bar kitchen. The majority look very similar in terms of design, but, the lower-cost pieces of equipment do have a far lower build quality. The good thing about fridges and freezers, though (unlike coffee machines), is there's not that much that can go wrong – in my experience it's only ever the condenser. With this in mind you should opt for low to mid range machines that are practical but not beautiful. Average prices fall around £1,200 per item.

☐ **Grab-and-go fridge** – Otherwise known as an 'open-fronted display chiller'. As with the serve-over counters, these vary massively in price, and size. For us, a 1.5 metre unit is sufficient to display drinks and chocolates, etc. New machines cost approximately £2,500, but you could pick up a good-quality second-hand one for around £800.

☐ **Contact grill** – Suitable for paninis, toasties, hot bacon, etc. In our experience a sandwich bar is best to invest in a good-quality domestic grill rather than a catering-grade machine. Domestic grills cost approx £45 and will last between six and nine months before needing to be replaced. The alternative, catering-grade griddle grills are four times the size, use up much more electricity and cost around £300. Suitable for a busy breakfast café, but unnecessary, we found, for our sandwich bar.

☐ **Smaller kitchen items** – Soup kettles, blenders, toasters, microwaves, etc. These are all less expensive individually but together still require a substantial initial outlay. Websites of catering suppliers like Nisbets (www.nisbets.co.uk) are great places to research up-to-date prices,

CASH VS LEASING

You'll have no doubt looked at the list of prices to expect and begun to question where all this money is going to come from? The answer is often found in leasing.

Most people have got used to the idea of leasing, or hire purchase. Many of us will have visited DFS and picked up a new sofa, delaying payment for two years, or have bought a new car using a payment scheme. The reason we choose these payment deals is that it frees up our cash, and enables us to purchase something we might otherwise not be able to afford to buy outright.

When buying equipment, fixtures and fittings for your new sandwich bar, the same rules apply, and you need to give some consideration to what you'll buy cash, and what you'll lease. You should bear in mind that you're probably going to have to subsidize your sandwich bar for a while, and your bank won't take too kindly to you requesting an increase to your overdraft facility a couple of months in, because you cash reserves are depleted.

Café Culture

Cash is king! When you start your business you need to ensure that you have as much as possible in the coffers, available to dip into, move around various bank accounts, pay for unexpected dips in sales, etc. For this reason we decided to use hire purchase as a way to buy much of our equipment. By factoring the anticipated monthly payments into our cash flow spreadsheet (see below) we were able to be confident that we could afford to meet the payments.

STRIKING THE RIGHT DEAL

Think about it like buying a car or a house. Generally, you don't go into a garage with no idea how much you're going to spend, or what you actually want the car for. Arthur Daley would have you for breakfast, and commercial appliance salespeople will treat you no differently, meaning that you'll probably walk away with a very expensive appliance you don't actually need.

Negotiation is actually a skill that most of us possess, but are too afraid to exercise for fear of 'looking silly'. This may be right in certain instances (you wouldn't haggle with your newsagent to lower the cost of your Mars bar), but it's certainly not the case here.

What is the right deal, then? Well, only you can answer that, as you know how important the piece of equipment will be to your business, how much you'll generate as a return on your investment and ultimately what you're willing to pay for it. As a general rule, people in sales market their products competitively, but with some room for manoeuvre. This means that you're never going to get them to give it away, but you should certainly expect some reduction in the price.

Here are some tips to help you seal the best deal:

  ☐ **Do your research.** Make sure you really understand the market, and know what products are available and at what price. Why are cheaper products cheaper, what additional functions do more expensive products have, what additional service and support do companies offer alongside the equipment? What do you need?

  ☐ **Decide what you want to spend.** Have a clear idea in your head of the price you want to pay for the equipment or service. Base this price on your research and be realistic. This price should be your silent goal, and all your negotiations should work towards achieving it.

  ☐ **The first offer.** Make sure that it's not ridiculously low. If you offer £150 for something priced at £700, the salesperson is not going to take you seriously; you'll show that you haven't done your research properly, and you may cause insult and damage the negotiations going forwards. Gauge what a fair price would be, and one that you'd be happy to settle on, and then make a first offer that is slightly below that.

  ☐ **Be firm and persistent.** Negotiation is like a game of cat and mouse. You have to work out how desperate the salesperson is to sell before you begin to push the price down. Consider whether the equipment or produce is end of line and perhaps needs to be sold quickly, or whether it's the end of the financial year and the salesperson is hoping to close as many deals as possible in a short space of time, or whether you intend to regularly buy produce from the company alongside the initial purchase of equipment.

'The right deal' is always going to be different for different businesses. The key is to know what is right for your business, and negotiate until you achieve it.

And remember, it's not always as cut and dried as achieving a discount off the list price. The salesperson may not be willing to reduce the cost of your coffee machine, but you could negotiate a free grinder, a box or two of syrups, a month's worth of coffee, etc. as part of the deal.

TOP TIP *how to books small business start-ups*

It's easy to be dazzled by futuristic, beautifully made Italian marble chiller counters. Yes, they'd look a million dollars in your café, but because they are handmade exclusively by a small number of suppliers, your chance of negotiating on price is very slim. You'll pay a fortune, and in our experience, as an independent you'll never achieve return on that initial investment.

Instead consider more generic equipment, sold by the majority of suppliers. You'll be able to play salespeople off against each other, to drive down the price – very important when opening your café on a budget.

To put this into perspective, when opening our first unit, we acquired approximately £5K worth of equipment for £4K, plus numerous 'freebies' such as coffee beans, syrups and milk steaming jugs.

WILL YOU BE VAT REGISTERED?

First, what is VAT? Value added tax, or VAT, is a tax charged on most business-to-business and business-to-consumer transactions in the UK. If you are a VAT registered business, VAT is a tax on the net value added to your products or services – the difference between the value of your sales and the value of your purchases. If you are a non-VAT registered businesses or organization, or a consumer, VAT is a tax on your consumption.

It is a legal requirement that your business is VAT registered if its turnover is over the threshold as set by the Chancellor. Currently this threshold is £67,000, but this figure changes annually so you should visit www.hmrc.gov.uk for up-to-date information.

The main question you need to ask yourself is, will your turnover be enough to warrant it? This is where things become tough, because you won't know what your anticipated turnover is until you forecast it. However, it's fair to say that in our experience the vast majority of café businesses would turnover in excess of the threshold figure.

Don't discount registering your business just because you think your annual turnover will be below the threshold (currently £67,000). There are benefits to being a VAT registered business, such as being able to claim VAT back on the various expenditures you make, such as rent, re-fit and equipment. Do your sums to make sure it's a worthwhile decision for you.

So, what can you expect once you are VAT registered? There are some specific VAT rules that relate to catering businesses, and these rules can be rather complicated and confusing. The major rules you need to understand are around the issues of whether food is sold for eat-in or takeaway, and whether it is hot or cold food.

VAT is not charged on cold food sold to be taken away. However, if that same cold food is sold to be consumed on the premises, then VAT is applied. All hot food, whether sold to be eaten on the premises or taken away, has VAT charged on it. You need to ensure that you keep clear and up-to-date records of all of these transactions, as they'll be required when you compile your VAT return at the end of the quarter.

Alongside these rules, being a VAT registered business does have its benefits. For example, when re-fitting your café, and buying equipment, it's very likely you will be charged VAT by builders, electricians, and refrigeration suppliers, etc. If your business is VAT registered, you will be able to claim back all the VAT you have been charged, within your first VAT return. For example, if you're spending £20,000 on various refrigeration equipment, the VAT you can anticipate claiming back will total about £3,000. A pretty handy reimbursement when your business is only a month or two old! In addition, you'll be able to claim the VAT back on your rent each month (if charged), which adds up to a fair amount each year.

I would highly recommend that you visit www.hmrc.gov.uk, and request copies of the government VAT guides, and also take advice from your accountant – it is vital that you get VAT right!

CASH FLOW FORECASTING

A large part of any business plan is cash flow forecasting, which in laypeople's terms simply means taking a long, hard and very realistic look at the numbers, in order to make sure that the business is going to be able to produce a reasonable profit.

As your sandwich bar is a new business venture it's accepted that your financial forecasts will be 'guesstimates'; however, these guesstimates are expected to be based on fact, and the thorough research you have undertaken.

Alarm Bell

Don't be tempted to massage the truth in order to impress those reading your business plan, such as banks and landlords. The person who'll be most hurt by this is YOU! After all, you're only fooling yourself, and if the business does not make money it'll be you that suffers. Do your research properly, and be honest with your financial forecasts.

In a nutshell, understanding your predicted cash flow is calculating exactly how much money you'll need to take per day/week to ensure that all your sandwich bar's bills are being paid, and that you have a salary for yourself.

Any independent adviser, investor, bank manager, landlord or supplier connected to your business will want to see that you have thoroughly worked through your cash flow forecasts and that your business is financially viable. Even if you don't require a bank loan to start your business, and have cash reserves to fund your shop re-fit or equipment purchase, it's still good practice to work out your forecast. After all, you surely want to know where your money is going, and to be certain that the investment you're about to make is a sound one?

UNDERSTANDING YOUR OUTGOINGS

Unless you're buying an existing business, you'll have absolutely no idea how many people will come into your shop, or how much they'll spend. That's the difficult part.

Use a computer programme such as Excel to develop your cash flow forecast. If you're new to computers, enrol yourself in a quick introduction course at your local adult learning college; you'll only need to understand the basics of creating spreadsheets. The main advantage of a computer-based system is that you'll be able to amend and save different versions as things change as you go along.

The best way to approach your financial forecasting is in reverse. It may seem strange working back to front, but you need to start with the facts you do know, not the ones that you don't. And so in this instance that's the costs you're going to incur in starting up and running your business.

Try following these simple steps.

☐ Create your cash flow spreadsheet (preferably in Excel). It should resemble a grid. In the left-hand column list all the costs you know your sandwich bar will have. This will include things like rent/mortgage, loan repayments, tax/NI, VAT (if applicable), staff wages. Then, along the top of the grid list the 12 months of the year.

☐ Don't forget to include your own mortgage, and basic living costs. Most people say they don't take a salary from their business in the early days, but unless you live mortgage free, and get through life by eating and drinking air, then you're going to need to cover your personal costs in some way. Be honest; build it into the cash flow forecast. Remember though, a bank adviser would be sorely disappointed in you if your 'personal costs' included holidays, facials and new cars. You're opening a new business, and any profit early on should be re-invested, not spent on treats. That comes later!

☐ Now start filling in the blanks. Begin with the details you already know. For example, from your earlier research you'll know that the annual rent for a shop unit the size you need in the town you're targeting is approximately £20K. So, now enter £1,700 into each month's box. Repeat the same exercise for all your known costs.

Alarm Bell

It's sensible always to overestimate rather than underestimate costs. That way you're always prepared for the worst-case scenario.

☐ Once all your costs are listed, you will have calculated your average monthly expenditure.

☐ To understand your sandwich bar's weekly expenditure, simply divide this monthly figure by four. This is the figure that you'll need to take through the till each week in order to break even. This means to pay all the bills, but not make any profit.

☐ Now, to understand how much you'll need to take per day, divide the weekly figure by the number of days you intend on trading for per week – five, six, seven?

Café Culture

Think of your cash flow spreadsheet as holding only the 'top line' information that's important to your business. The bank doesn't want to know how much each of your fridges will cost, but does want a realistic figure for your sandwich bar's overall fixtures and fittings.

We have separate spreadsheets set up for more detailed figures, such as indiviual fixtures and fittings. We use these to drill down and understand the detailed costings, and only the total is then included within the cash flow forecast.

CALCULATING REALISTIC INCOMINGS

You now have a clear starting point for your cash flow forecasting. You know how much it'll cost you to open your business and trade. Now you need to work out whether this figure is realistic. Let's say that daily figure is £500.

Average spend per head – in other words, the average amount each of your customers will spend when they visit your sandwich bar – will very much depend on your proposition. For example, if your sandwich bar is primarily sit down and eat in then average spend will be higher than if it is takeaway. For this exercise let's base your customer's average spend on a worker's lunch of a sandwich, a bag of crisps and a coffee: total spend of approx £5 (sandwich £2.50, crisps 50p, coffee £2).

In order to break even, and take the £500 you need to each day, you're going to have to serve 100 customers, all spending £5. Now, over the course of a day that doesn't sound like a lot of people, but remember, lunch generally lasts for two hours, and that period will generate roughly 75% of your total takings.

That means that you'll need to serve 75 people between 12 noon and 2pm. That's one customer every 90 seconds, continually for two hours straight. Sounds a bit more challenging now, doesn't it?

Are there enough potential customers within a three-minute walk of your sandwich bar to enable you to serve 100 per day? If you're planning on being located near to a large office block with, say, 1,000 staff, are you confident that you'll attract one in ten of the workers every single day? Will you be the only sandwich bar option for customers, or will you have lots of competition, all taking their slice of the cake?

Obviously your hope is that your sales figure is going to rise after a few months, but don't think this will happen quickly. Even a couple of years into our first venture, customers were coming in saying, they hadn't noticed us before!

After four to five months you should pencil in an incremental change to the sales (don't forget to change the expenditure column as well, as you'll be buying more bread, more milk, etc.) based on what you anticipate sales to rise to, but also what you can physically deliver. If you're looking at a small operation with approximately 200 sq ft, then you're not going to be able to service 300 customers effectively. Know your limits, and don't over-exaggerate anything. Be very honest with these figures, as you'll only be kidding yourself. As sales increase, you'll also need to increase staff wages to service customers' needs.

If, a few months in, you're forecasting daily takings of £700, don't forget that the extra £200 isn't pure profit. Your margin on the £200 is the profit, as you'll have the extra labour and produce to pay for. It's your money, but in the early days you should re-invest this money into the business, and get it on solid ground as early as possible, rather than buying a new BMW! For every good day there'll always be a quieter day round the corner, and as a business owner you should be continually prepared for a slight dip in sales.

Setting up your business

You could serve the best food and drink in the UK, and have a sandwich bar full to the rafters with hungry people every minute of every day, but if you haven't got your business head screwed on it'll all be in vain. Getting the structure and framework of your business right, and choosing the right professionals to work for you, should be your top priorities.

PARTNERING FOR SUCCESS

Going into business is hard work, and there's certainly a lot to be said for sharing the various burdens with a partner. After all, you'd each bring different skills and experience, you'd be able to share the physically demanding workload, and provide holiday cover for each other. You'd also be able to brainstorm new ideas and undoubtedly come up with many more solutions to problems when they rise.

However, a small business such as a sandwich bar is often simply not big or profitable enough to accommodate the ideas and financial requirements of two separate owners. I think this is the reason why most successful sandwich bar partnerships I have encountered are of husbands and wives. They have all the benefits of sharing the burden of ownership, but with only one household needing to take an income.

Café Culture

My husband Richard and I are business partners. The reason our business relationship works is because we each have clearly defined areas of ownership, just as all workers do in their jobs. I am responsible for the food and kitchen, human resources and marketing, and Richard is responsible for financial management, new business and business expansion.

DECIDING ON THE LEGAL STRUCTURE

You need to decide what form your sandwich bar business will take. You have a choice of the following.

Sole trader

Many independent sandwich bars operate under sole trader status. The reason is that it's relatively straightforward in terms of registration, record-keeping and paperwork. It's also significantly less expensive, because as a sole trader you are entitled to keep all your profits after tax. In addition a sole trader is not required to make public any information about the business. This limits accountancy fees, as no annual report has to be written.

However, as there is no distinction between you as an individual and the business you own, you are personally liable to pay all costs should your sandwich bar fail. This means your own possessions, including your home and car, could be at risk if you can't pay your business debts.

You do not need to notify Companies House if you are operating as a sole trader. However, you do need to notify the Inland Revenue within three months, or suffer the penalty fine of £100 (www.inlandrevenue.co.uk). You'll also need to ensure that you keep a record of all your business's income and outgoings. In addition, although sole traders are often taxed as self-employed, this isn't always the case, so you'll need to notify HM Revenue & Customs within three months of starting up to ensure you're paying your tax correctly.

Partnership

A partnership is as it sounds: an agreement between two or more people to go into business together. It could be as informal as a handshake, or as formal as a detailed legal document. Partnerships allow you to share the responsibility of running the business, and may also be a way to pool resources. However, the most important thing to realize if you are considering forming a partnership is that partners are liable for the debts of the business. So, if your sandwich bar fails, or your partner runs out on you, you'll be left to pay for everything out of your own pocket. This again would mean your own possessions are at risk.

The key is to make sure that you create a formal agreement (ideally with the help of a solicitor), and ensure that it includes the following details:

☐ How the business is to be financed.

☐ How the profits will be split.

☐ How the losses will be split.

☐ What happens if one of the partners decides to leave.

Also discuss who'll take responsibility for which areas of the business. Will one be in charge of the bookkeeping and banking, while the other is managing the day-to-day running of the café, food and staff? Decision-making can take longer than necessary and there can be difficulties agreeing if roles are not clearly defined from the outset. That said, two heads can be better than one, and it's beneficial to have someone to share the burden of a new business.

It's far easier to decide these details at the beginning, than later, if things don't go to plan.

Alarm Bell

If you are forming a partnership with your husband or wife consider the implications should you divorce.

Limited liability partnership

Limited liability partnerships (LLP) are relatively new. They share many of the features of normal partnerships, but also offer reduced personal responsibility for business debt. Members of an LLP have their own personal liability limited to the amount of money they themselves invested in the business, and to any personal guarantees they may have given in order to raise funds for the business.

However, forming an LLP is far more complicated and expensive than simply forming a partnership. You have to send a registration form to Companies House, which costs £20, and you would certainly need to employ a solicitor to establish a partnership agreement outlining how the LLP will be run and how profits will be shared.

In addition to this your business would have higher running costs. One reason for this would be that you'd be required to make financial information about your company public by sending your annual accounts to Companies House, something that an accountant would need to manage for you.

Members of an LLP are often taxed as self-employed, although this isn't always the case.

Limited liability company (Ltd)

When you form a limited liability company, you create a business in its own right, not simply an extension of yourself. This means that as the owner you are less at risk. If your sandwich bar were being sued (e.g. for matters relating to food hygiene, or a staff injury), this would mean that the business faced the judges, not you as an individual. If you decide to set up a limited company you would not only be lowering your financial liability, you would be ensuring that the company would continue should anything happen to you. Important to remember if you have a family.

Setting up as a limited company gives you the opportunity to raise money by allowing individuals or other businesses to subscribe for shares in the company. It enables you to offer employees the opportunity to own a share in the business. Operating as a company also brings credibility, and many suppliers, and potential customers, will see it as a mark of professionalism and trustworthiness.

Alarm Bell

An LLP or limited company approach will not safeguard you entirely from the risks of financial losses. As a director of a new company you'll need to provide personal guarantees for any money that you loan, or leases that you agree to. So, while your personal financial liability will be lower than it would as a sole trader, it will still be a threat.

This is the unfortunate downside of starting up your own business. You're taking a risk, and putting yourself, and your processions on the line. Make sure you're 100% sure your business will work!

However, on the negative side it is important not to underestimate the increased paperwork required of a limited company, such as the annual returns required by companies House (an accountant will need to file these for you). You will also be liable to pay additional tax via corporation tax.

To set up as a limited company you will be required to give your company a name, have a UK address for your registered office, and have at least one director and a company secretary.

You can choose to deal directly with Companies House (www.companieshouse. co.uk) or employ a local solicitor or accountant. Or hire a specialist company to set up the formation of your new company for you, such as Quick Formations (www.quickformations. co.uk). They will manage the process from beginning to end, and create your Memorandum and Articles of Association. These can also be bought in template form from legal stationers.

Café Culture

We decided to form a limited liability company, partly because there are two of us, partly because we deal with food and there could be some risk of liability there, and partly because our plan was to grow our company beyond our first shop. We chose to use an accountant to form our limited company. He charged £100, and undertook all the paperwork related to the formation of Taste (UK) Ltd through Companies House.

Make the most of the free advice available to new business start-ups.

- **England and Northern Ireland – www.busineslink.gov.uk**
- **Wales – www.business-support-wales.gov.uk**
- **Scotland – www.bgateway.com**

You can also contact your local Chamber of Commerce, who'll have a new business adviser ready to answer your questions.

SECURING FUNDING – LOANS

You don't need to audition for *Dragons' Den*, but you will need to apply some of the same skills employed in this show, as you try to convince someone to lend you a large hunk of cash.

If you already have a personal account with one of the big four, (HSBC, Barclays, Lloyds TSB, NatWest), then your bank is the best place to start. Arrange an appointment with a business adviser to see what kind of funding they may be able to offer you. Your own bank is going to be better to start with as they know your financial history, and can see how you manage your own personal money. Conversely, if you're forever overdrawn, and incurring fees, then it's probably better to start elsewhere! (I would also recommend you get yourself in order, and really question whether you have the skills required to run your own business.)

Once you've worked out your forecasts, calculate how much actual cash (different from leasing equipment) you need in order to open up. Take a look at this figure, and compare it with how much you're investing from your own pocket. If you're only investing £2K, and you're asking to borrow £100K, the bank will very politely tell you to go back to the dreamland you came from! As a general rule, most banks will want to see around 10% investment from the business owner, alongside a very strong business plan.

If you do only have a small amount available to fund the start of your business, then you may need to consider scaling down your operation accordingly. Economic conditions are also a very significant factor, and something you must bear in mind when speaking to people in the banking sector. If the economy is grinding to a halt, you're going to have to work much harder to convince someone to lend you any money.

So, you've booked your appointment with the banks adviser/consultant. What next? Now the hard work starts. You need to go through your cash flow forecasts and business plan with a fine-tooth comb to ensure the numbers add up. Ensure you are confident that you will be able to answer any questions in a calm and reassuring manner. Being either cocky or vague is definitely not recommended.

Think about it. If you went out to dinner with two friends, and when the cheque came they both realized they had forgotten their wallets, who would you sub money to? The trustworthy one who explained that they had simply left their wallet in the car, and promised that they'd transfer the money they owed you the next morning, or the one who lives life by the seat of their pants, unsure whether they have any cash, when they get paid, and when they can pay you back?

There are, of course, a whole host of other people who will lend you money, but in the same vein as *Dragons' Den*, they will want a large slice of your pie. If you're happy to relinquish parts of your pie, then that's a route to go, and Business Link will be able to put you in touch with lots of companies that specialize in this area.

In our view, though, as a one-shop, independent café, you will not make enough profit to support yourself and your family, and also provide an outside share-holder with a return.

USING PROFESSIONAL HELP

No matter how experienced you are, you're going to need professional help in order to run your business. In our view, the most successful small business owners accept what they're not so good at, and hire help in that area. After all, you wouldn't start mixing cement and laying bricks if you wanted to build your own house. The same principles apply here. And while you may well feel that paying professionals is money down the drain, when it comes to running your business, it is in fact one of the best investments you'll make.

Unless you have existing relationships with a solicitor or accountant, my best suggestion is to meet with two or three of each, and then go with the one that best suits your needs. (Not always the cheapest!)

Solicitors

As with any sizeable transaction, you'll need to appoint a legal representative to act on your behalf. This legal representative is your solicitor, and you'll be seeing a lot of them in the early days of your business. They will deal with the legal structure of your business, and the lease or purchase of your property.

Where to start? As always, consider personal recommendations, so ask around. Then take a look along your local high street; many firms have offices located above shops, etc. You can also contact the Law Society (www.lawsociety.org.uk), who keep a register of solicitors with expertise in particular areas.

Next, telephone two or three local firms and arrange an initial meeting. Explain that you are setting up a new business, that you need to appoint a solicitor to handle your business affairs, and that you'd like to come in for an initial chat to find out about the services the firm offers and the pricing structure.

Consider the speed and efficiency of this initial communication with the firm. Was the meeting arranged quickly and without fuss? Were your calls returned? When you visited the office did it look organized? Did you find the person you met with to be helpful? Did he or she make time for you, or did you feel rushed? Were they able to give examples of other small business clients they work with?

These are all very important points to consider. The solicitor you choose will play a critical role in the smooth opening of your business. Choose one that is overloaded with work, disorganised or inexperienced and your shop opening could easily end up being delayed by two or three months, due to overrunning legal matters.

From the outset, ensure that your solicitor agrees to a completion date. Your job as the client is then to be in constant communication with your solicitor, pushing the deal forwards as quickly as possible. You need to be focused, and unrelenting – do not let the pace slow. You might even want to agree the solicitor's fee based on them having completed the legal works by a certain date.

Accountants

Although often jokingly dubbed dull and grey, these guys are in fact going to be your best friend throughout your entire business life. They'll advise you on matters such as:

☐ How you structure your company (sole trader, limited company, etc.)

☐ Paying tax (and in fact paying as little as legitimately possible)

☐ Personal tax for you (and your partner)

☐ VAT

☐ PAYE and National Insurance

☐ Tax, tax rates, self-assessment, etc.

☐ Annual reports to Companies House (if you're a limited company)

☐ Capital gains (if you sell the business).

Café Culture

We stuck rigidly to the timeline prior to opening our first café. This is because we knew that any delay to opening would cost money – money that we simply did not have. Frustratingly, however, our solicitor at the time did not seem to have the same sense of urgency when it came to the legal documents relating to the lease of the shop unit we were taking on. Our calls would not be returned, deadlines would slip, and communication was appalling.

In the end I stepped in, and acted as the go-between between our solicitor and the solicitor acting on behalf of the landlord. Time was of the essence, so we didn't care whether this was an unusual way of doing things. We simply wanted the deal done, so that our builders could commence the re-fit.

We logged an official complaint with the firm of solicitors we used, as we felt that the customer service they had provided was second-rate. We also negotiated a reduction to the final invoice for the work they carried out. Don't be afraid to complain. Solicitors should provide you with just as high a level of service as any other professionals, and if they don't then you should be compensated.

Most sandwich bars will have relatively small-scale accountancy requirements, so often this kind of work will be suited to an individual accountant or a small high street practice. As always, you should consider personal recommendations when seeking an accountant, and use www.yell.com to search for those located in your local area.

Repeat the exercise you carried out when seeking a solicitor. Telephone two or three local firms and arrange an initial meeting. Explain that you are setting up a new business, that you will be appointing an accountant, and that you'd like to come in for an initial chat to find out about the services the firm offers and the pricing structure.

Again, consider the speed and efficiency of communication, whether you found the accountant helpful and knowledgeable, and whether they were able to give examples of other small business clients they work with.

FINDING A BANK

When it comes to small business banking, the big four (Lloyds TSB, Barclays, NatWest and HSBC) are all pretty much the same. They tend to offer similar deals in terms of free banking for new start-ups. Again, my best suggestion is to see at least these four before deciding which you'll bank with.

Café Culture

We found our accountant on www.yell.com and she's proved to be a perfect match for our business. She works on her own, and has a handful of local business clients. As Richard is comfortable keeping our accounts, we have kept the annual records in-house, meaning that we keep our accounting costs to a minimum. Our accountant produces the annual reports required by Companies House, due to our limited company status. She also manages our monthly payroll transactions, and our tax assessments.

Don't just choose one because you personally bank with them. When we first opened we chose Lloyds TSB because they were offering the longest period of free banking. Once this period was up, we switched to HSBC for a further six months' worth of free banking. Depending on your turnover, free banking could save you up to £200 per month!

If you decide that you will be accepting electronic payment from customers, you will have to set up a different type of bank account, called a merchant account, and this account needs to be held by an 'acquiring bank'. Most of the big high street banks fall into this category. You'll need to establish suitable procedures and take advice from your bank to minimize risk of fraud.

When and how to take the leap

Finally deciding to hand in your resignation is indeed a big step to take. However, there will come a time when you can no longer juggle the demands of work with those of your infant business, and you'll be forced to make a commitment. For those going it alone, without the support of a partner's salary this can be a frightening prospect. However, quitting the nine to five need not be as cut and dried as you might think.

Consider being candid with your employer. Explain your plans, and that you intend to tender your resignation in the coming months. Perhaps suggest that you begin by shortening your working week, to say three days, giving you three days to work at home on your business (always try and have one day off per week). Many employers might welcome this, as it gives them longer to recruit a suitable replacement. You may also be able to quit but continue to do some sporadic freelance days, when your previous employer needs help with extra workload. Consider all your options, and do your best to keep the money flowing into your account; you'll need all the cash you can earn.

For us, as partners, we were able to stagger our resignations, in order to ensure that we had at least one salary per month during the research and development of our café. Richard left his job five months before we opened, and then carried out some ad hoc freelance work to keep the money coming in. I worked until the end of March, six weeks before our scheduled opening date of 8 May. We sold our nice car, turned down invites to dinners out with friends, we waved goodbye to expensive weekly shops at Waitrose. It wasn't until the ten-month point that we could tentatively begin spending on ourselves again, and treat ourselves to the odd night away. And we drove around in an old banger for just over a year. You need to be prepared for this, financially and emotionally.

Finding your premises

Location, location, location. The old adage does not just apply to houses. You've no doubt heard of, or perhaps visited, a 'destination' pub or restaurant – one that is a lengthy drive away, but you are prepared to make the effort to visit it because of the reputation, food on offer or award-winning status.

Ever heard of a 'destination' sandwich bar? No. That's because they simply don't exist. Regardless of how delicious your food is, how friendly your staff are, or how beautiful your café is, your customers simply will not travel off the beaten track to find you. Why? Because breakfast and lunchtime food is all about convenience. People want to fit their food purchase into their already busy day, not make it even more hectic.

Alarm Bell

Do not underestimate how hard it will be to find a suitable site for your sandwich bar. Too begin with, it'll be difficult to find a unit that ticks all your boxes. Then agents won't return your calls, because your business is new and they've got bigger businesses with brand names looking for retail units. You may find that landlords are reluctant to lease premises to new businesses with no track record. And it's likely that the likes of Subway and Costa have grabbed many of the good high street units already.

It can be done, but you'll need masses of determination.

ESTABLISHING A BRIEF

Your brief should be based on your business plan, and what you hope your sandwich bar will be like. For example, if you're planning to open a takeaway sandwich bar, for office workers, then you need a smaller unit, approximately 500–700 sq ft in size, with an A1 licence. You'll also need to ensure that the shop is on the doorstep of an office district. However, if your plan is to open a delicatessen café, and you intend your customers to be affluent with more leisure time, people who like to chill over a hunk of cake and a long coffee, then it is probable you'll need more like 2,000 sq ft, an A3 licence, and for the shop to be located on an up-market high street.

All retail units have been categorized into various usage licences, including A1, A2, A3, or mixed use.

The parameters of these licences can be somewhat blurred, as they are often interpreted by the individual area planning officer. However, it's fair to say that a takeaway only sandwich bar could operate from an A1 licence, whereas a café with many tables and serving a high percentage of hot food such as soup and jackets could require an A3 licence.

I'd recommend that you get in touch with your local council planning officer as early as possible, be open about the plans for your business, and get an understanding of what they would permit.

There are more A1 retail units available than A3, so at this stage you may decide to tweak your plans so that you can operate under an A1 licence.

UNDERTAKING RECONNAISSANCE

The first step in your research is to get organized. Buy a large foldable map of your local area and pin it up on your sandwich shop HQ wall. Then decide how wide your search zone is going to be, taking into account how long it'll take you to get to work. In our experience it is sensible to be no more than

41

35 minutes' drive away from your sandwich bar, due to early mornings, long days and possible emergency call-outs.

Next, make a list of all the possible locations where you could base your sandwich bar. This should not be too hard, as you'll have already begun to form some opinions of locations based on your early research into the sandwich bar market, and other cafés. There'll also be some locations that you're keen to visit due to regeneration, redevelopment, and gut instinct. You may need to think outside the box here; most of the good locations will have already been taken, as the 'food to go' market has expanded over the past ten years.

Consider parts of towns and cities where previously a sandwich bar might not have been viable: in an up-and-coming neighbourhood, or close to a new business park or trading estate. Also consider streets that are close by a popular and expensive high street location. This is often a sensible way to get the best of both worlds. As long as you entice people in, through well-positioned 'A' boards advertising your café, you could end up with a high footfall but a lower rent.

Café Culture

Our first unit had been empty for two years prior to us signing the lease. It is located on a busy road in a town centre, but it is off the beaten track for shoppers visiting the indoor mall. We spotted, however, that it was on the main thoroughfare for office workers walking from the office district into the town for lunch. In fact, it was the first shop they came to on their route. The rent was relatively low because of the shop's secondary location, but we were happy to take the risk because we knew the footfall and had researched the market. We ended up with a reasonable rent and an excellent level of passing trade. And the shoppers soon found us, once they'd begun to hear of our excellent reputation!

Now make a checklist of the key factors that you'll consider when viewing a retail unit. Ask yourself the following:

☐ Does it fit the brief? Are your target customers in this area?

☐ Is there passing trade? Is the road a busy thoroughfare, on a bus route, near the station? Is it a high street with popular shops? Is the shop high visibility or hidden away?

☐ Is there a captive audience? No matter what your business plan, the lunchtime trade is a vital one for any sandwich bar. To be a success you'll need to tap into one of two captive audiences (or both if your location is prime!): first, office workers who tend to buy their lunch out three or four times per week, and second, shoppers, who'll visit you less frequently, but will spend more per visit.

Alarm Bell

Beware! Think about the consistency of trade. For example, if the location relies heavily on students, could your business cope with the several months of the year when they are on holiday and not spending money in your café? Are there any plans to redirect traffic, to change bus routes? Will this affect the passing trade?

□ **Are there any competitors?** As the likes of Subway and Costa have been busy securing a foothold on almost every British high street, it's very unlikely that you'll find no competitors. In fact, if there were no competitors it's probably a clear sign not to bother with the area. You need to understand what your competition would be like if you chose this site. It's OK if there are a couple of places, offering different types of food, but if there are already a number of sandwich bars offering what you plan to offer then it's probably best to look elsewhere.

Café Culture

When we opened in May 2006 there were numerous competitors within a five-minute walk of our new shop. This included some independent sandwich bars, together with national chains such as O'Brien's, Greggs (x3), Costa (x2), Starbucks and Benjis. We worked hard to differentiate ourselves, and to sell on our unique food offering. Two years later we were established, and winning awards, while O'Brien's, Benjis and a couple of independents had closed down.

□ **Is there potential for outside seating?** The smoking ban has made business difficult for some, while on the other hand it has created an opportunity for others. Don't discount the importance of having one or two outside tables, with shelter from sun or rain.

Café Culture

When we viewed our first unit in December 2005 we were aware of the impending smoking ban, and so were hoping to find a unit with the capacity to offer some outside seating. Our shop had an outside undercover walkway, and with permission granted by the council to install tables and chairs it made the perfect smokers' seating area. Now, most of our mid-morning trade is thanks to this seating area and it contributes heavily to our turnover.

☐ **Are the logistics workable?** Does the premises have ample parking for you and your staff? Will your customers require parking? Can delivery drivers stop and unload? Is there somewhere to put rubbish for collection? If you intend to have a van, and make sandwich deliveries, is there somewhere to stop and load? Is the shop based on a traffic blocked one-way system?

Consider developing a scorecard for each retail unit you view. Grade each one out of ten, across the above points and any others that are specific to your business plan. It could prove to be a really useful tactic, and mean that you can be confident of whether the unit offered has potential or not.

PURCHASE OR LEASE?

This should be one of the shortest sections in this book. As, due to the generally safe option of investing money in bricks and mortar, if at all feasible the sensible answer should always be purchase! After all, if you buy a retail unit it will usually increase in value as the years go by, providing you with a nice nest-egg many years from now.

Purchase

You'll find that retail units in good locations don't become available to purchase very often, as landlords generally don't have trouble renting them out, and simply keep their property portfolio bubbling over. However, if you think you may have found a gem of a unit to purchase, check, double-check, triple-check, and then do it all over again until you're completely satisfied you're happy with the terms and condition of the unit.

Ask yourself, if this unit is so great, why are they selling it? There may be a genuine reason such as bereavement, or a small landlord management company closing its portfolio. This is very rare, though, and if *you* are aware of the unit's availability, so too are the big property developers and landlord companies.

Why don't they want it? After all, they will have ongoing relationships with national agents and will know about such units before they come on to the open market. Don't be naive; there will be a reason why this unit is not attractive to large landlord firms. You need to discover what the reason is, and decide whether it's a deal-breaker for you and your business.

The truth is, though, that not many start-up sandwich bar owners have the cash available to purchase a retail unit in a high footfall high street location . . . so this section suddenly becomes much longer!

Leasing

Leasing is the chosen route for the vast majority of retailers, from large chains through to small independents. There are far more leasehold retail units to choose from, and a smaller deposit is required to purchase a lease than to purchase a mortgage. However, the research you should undertake before deciding to lease a property should be just as thorough as when deciding to purchase a property. After all, you'll be responsible for paying the rent for as long as your lease is valid, regardless of whether your business is a success or a failure.

Once you've made the decision, and are confident that the unit can offer you all that you need to make your business a success, then you'll begin negotiating a full repairing and insuring lease (FRI). An FRI lease is the usual format of lease used within retail, and simply means the person leasing the property (you) is responsible for the general repair and insuring of the unit.

No two retail leases are the same, as there will always be individual clauses relating to particular premises. For example, a retail landlord in one high street may ensure that all of their FRI leases contain a clause outlawing the sale of any hot food from premises trading under an A1 licence. However, if the only hot food you intend to sell is toasted sandwiches and jacket potatoes, you may be able to negotiate this into the contract.

The important thing is to ensure that you have a very good solicitor, who will study the lease and all relating legal documentation with a fine-tooth comb, making sure that nothing is missed, and there are no nasty clauses waiting to bite you in two years' time.

As well as agreeing to the terms of the lease, you'll also agree to the length of the lease. You should expect this to be for anywhere between five and 20 years. The landlord will usually specify how long they wish the lease period to be for, and this is generally non-negotiable.

Café Culture

We knew of a business that began trading as a delicatessen. After a while the owners realized that they could not make sufficient profits to support their overheads, and so they introduced the sale of sandwiches and coffee in order to increase turnover. The café side of their business did relatively well, and they increased the number of tables and chairs in order to serve more customers.

However, they did not realize that their lease did not allow the consumption of food and drink on the premises. The landlord was unhappy, and demanded that they return to their original business plan, as a deli. They could not sustain themselves on this limited income, and six months later they closed down for good.

The lesson here is to ensure that you are happy with the terms of your lease, and that you understand the restrictions it could place on your business.

MAKING AN OFFER AND NEGOTIATING A DEAL

As leasing is the option the vast majority of retailers take, I'll focus on this, rather than on purchasing a property. Once you have decided that a property is suitable for your business, you will begin the process of making an offer and negotiating the deal.

Heads of terms

The first step is to request a document known as the 'heads of terms' (HoT) from the property agent. This document holds the basic contractual information relating to the property lease, including the length of lease, annual rent, any service charge that is applicable, length of any rent-free period, and the usage licence relating to the property (A1, A2, A3, etc.).

As the average retail lease is over 100 pages long, the purpose of the HoT is to provide an executive summary, so that all parties can agree on the top-line details, and be certain that they want to progress, before beginning to negotiate the intricate details of the lease contract in its entirety.

If you are negotiating with a large national landlord firm then this HoT will be a formal document, one or two pages long. On the other hand if you are dealing with a small local landlord then you may simply receive a brief email. The important thing is that you receive these details, and that you ensure you are happy with them.

This is your opportunity to negotiate on the amount of annual rent you'll pay, rent-free period you would like, the length of the lease, the usage of the lease, etc. It's important to view the bigger picture when negotiating, and remember that it's not simply about getting a cheaper annual rent.

Added value at this stage could be of real benefit to your business in the longer term. For example, the landlord may not be able to reduce the annual rent; however, they may offer added value in the form of rent free periods, reduced service charges, a free rubbish collection, a free parking space, etc.

Café Culture

When starting up, cash is king. So, when negotiating for our first unit we decided to offer the asking price, but push really hard on the rent-free period and other extras. We managed to squeeze seven months rent-free from the landlord, which meant that if we kept our re-fit within the four-week target we would have the first six months of trading rent-free. What a great foot to get your business off on, and relieve some pressure.

The general rule of thumb is that a three-months rent-free period is granted when taking a lease. However, negotiate hard, and you may come out with more. In addition, if the unit you are leasing is in a poor state of repair and the re-fit you are undertaking is likely to be lengthy and expensive, negotiate a longer rent-free period to recompense you for the investment you'll be making.

The contract

Once you have agreed the HoT (a process that may take a few weeks) the next step is to instruct your solicitor to begin work on the contract itself. Much like buying a house, this process can be a lengthy one and you should anticipate it taking at least two or three months.

Your solicitor will handle the negotiation of the contract from this point onwards, and act as your representative. It is therefore vital that you have explained to them in detail the exact plans you have for your business. For example, your plan may be to sell cold sandwiches for takeaway, but will your business stay like this for ever, or might its offering change slightly as the years go by? You need to ensure that your solicitor knows this, so that they can make sure that the contract is flexible enough to fit your requirements.

As well as ensuring your solicitor is thoroughly briefed on your business plan you'll need to ensure that they understand the deadlines you are working to. If you need to have the keys to the shop and have begun the re-fit by a certain date, then say so, and demand that your solicitor works to meet this deadline. Your job is to be a firm taskmaster, and make sure they prioritize your workload.

From the point of requesting HoT to the day you start trading, you should allow approx six months.

Creating your brand identity

What kind of food do you sell? What service can a customer expect? What do you excel in? These are all important questions that customers want answers to, before they come into your sandwich bar. But how do you answer these questions and tempt them in? The answer is with your brand, otherwise known as your company's image and character.

The reason I propose that you spend time developing your brand now, before you even begin to source suppliers or fit out your premises, is because once you have a brand image set for your business you'll have a clear reference point for all the decisions to come. For example, when deciding which snacks to stock, which tables and chairs to buy, whether your staff should wear a uniform, you need simply ask yourself, is this in keeping with my brand image?

But what makes up a brand? Here are eight essential elements that added together will make up your sandwich bar's identity:

1. Name

2. Key message

3. Logo

4. Packaging

5. Advertising

6. Promotions

7. Promotional materials

8. Publicity

At this stage it's important to concentrate on points 1–3. We'll cover points 4–8 in Chapter 3, when you're preparing to open for business.

Take a moment now to think about the companies you know and have a strong understanding of. Take Marks & Spencer and British Airways, or perhaps ASDA and Easy Jet. These firms are all very different, – yet they also have one thing in common, a strong brand. As consumers we instinctively know what to expect from these companies, whether that is high-quality produce and customer service, or affordability and practicality. They do not confuse us; we're clear about what it is they offer us and whether it's for us. That's because they have employed the eight essential elements to their advantage.

It's true that these firms have spent many years and hundreds of millions of pounds developing their brand. It's also true that no independent sandwich bar owner could compete with this level of investment! However, there is no reason why, on a far smaller budget, and with a little imagination, you can't create a strong brand all of your own.

Alarm Bell

Get it right and you'll be a 'brand' name in your own town, just as recognized as Costa, Starbucks, etc. Get it wrong and you'll be overlooked, and miss out on the chance to wow customers coming in through your door.

CHOOSING YOUR SANDWICH BAR NAME

The old adage 'it's all in a name' isn't actually that true, but it does play a pretty important part in the equation. The name you choose for your sandwich bar should communicate what you're all about; it should be easy to spell, to say and to memorize. Don't opt for foreign words that people can't pronounce, or try to be too clever or funny with abbreviations or word plays. Many people simply won't 'get it'.

Your name should also be as ageless as possible, and should not tie you down to a particular food type or concept. For example, imagine you called your business The Bagel Bar, then three months in you find that actually bagels are not that popular and so you start concentrating more on baguettes and wraps. You'd be faced with the choice of re-branding your business, something that is costly to you and confusing to the customer, or carrying on with a name that's no longer relevant to your business, and again confusing the customer!

Café Culture

I know of a café that's named after the Italian verb for 'let's eat'. In three years I have not once heard a customer refer to it by name. This is because people are not confident of how to pronounce the foreign word. The café often ends up being referred to as 'that place by Halifax bank', or simply 'the café'.

If you don't already have a name or two in mind, try having a brainstorm with a small group of trusted friends; I would suggest no more than five people. Provide them each with a paragraph describing what your sandwich bar or café will be like, the kind of food you'll concentrate on serving, what kind of things you want to communicate. Have your mood board and clippings and the menus you've collected on display to stimulate debate. Then get people to say the first things that come into their head, while you jot it all down. Don't discount anything immediately; your aim is to keep the conversation flowing. Once everyone has left, go through your notes and highlight interesting and relevant words and phrases that you think fit well with your brand. Can any be turned into imaginative and straightforward names for your business?

Check whether your chosen name is already being used. Search the Companies House website to see if any limited companies are using it, and look in the local phone book and online. Check too with the Patent Office, to see if the name has been trademarked. This saves hassle, especially later, if you decide to become a limited company.

It's important to remember too, that no matter what name your sandwich bar trades under (e.g. The Bread Basket), if you are operating as a sole trader you are required to display your own name and address in the café and on stationery.

DEVELOPING YOUR KEY MESSAGE

Communicating with your target customers is not rocket science. It's simply about having clear messages, that are relevant to them, and that you repeat again, and again and again. The first thing you need to do is to develop one, two, or perhaps a maximum of three, key messages about your business.

Once you've decided on a name, protect it.

Whether you intend to have a website or not, you should register your domain name. You can do this by visiting sites such as www.1and1.co.uk or www.easyspace.com. Registering your domain name and renting the online space will cost you anywhere from £9.99 to £35 per year. Your 'domain name' is the bit that goes in between the 'www' and '.co.uk' or '.com'

Register your name with the National Business Register www.anewbusiness.co.uk and Companies House www.companieshouse.gov.uk.

You can develop these messages by considering two important points. First, consider your USP (unique selling point). You decided upon this when writing your business plan. It's the foods or services that you discovered you'd need to offer in order to differentiate your sandwich bar from its competitors. Second, consider your audience. You also decided upon this when writing your business plan. Your audience is the group of people you decided to target; they are the customers you will concentrate on attracting into your café.

For example, through your research did you discover a gap in the market for a sandwich bar that could boast using freshly roasted joints of meat, instead of bought-in sliced cuts? Did you also note that a large proportion of the local office worker community is highly paid men? Your aim now is to develop a set of key messages designed to communicate what your sandwich bar offers that's special and, importantly, that's going to excite your target audience. So, considering the audience – highly paid mainly men, working in an office: strapped for time but not for cash – your key message could look something like this:

☐ 'Smith's' sandwich bar – freshly roasted British meats, prepared with care.

Additional messages you could use to communicate with this audience might include:

☐ Sandwiches, baguettes, subs and salads, all made fresh with our home-roasted meats.

☐ Fresh and filling food, handmade quickly to order.

Once you've created your key message, it should be communicated to your customers at every possible opportunity. On window posters, in promotional flyers, on your shop sign, on staff T-shirts. Repeat, repeat and repeat again!

CREATING YOUR LOGO

You've decided on your sandwich bar's name, and your key message(s). The next step is to create its logo. Think of this as an emblem that will come to signify all that your sandwich bar represents. Your logo could be a picture, an illustration, or simply your company name in a particular type font.

As well as a shape, you will need to consider which colours reflect your brand personality and appeal to your target audience. Colours tend to convey the following:

☐ Red, orange and yellow – energy, excitement and interest

☐ Neutrals – confidence

☐ Blue and green – stable and calming

☐ Bright green – freshness

☐ Brown – earthy, wholesome

In the case of our example sandwich bar 'Smith's, a colour combination of brown and red might be a good choice. This is because Smith's is targeting mainly highly paid men, who care about the quality of the food they eat, but who are busy and need rapid service at lunchtime.

The logo you choose will eventual appear on all your branding, marketing and promotional material. This will include shop signs, business cards, letter-headed paper, labels, carrier bags, vans, aprons, menus, posters, leaflets, website, etc.

DIY VS DESIGNER

Some small business owners make a great job of coming up with a snappy and rel-evant name and an eye-catching and professional logo without the help of a professional graphic designer. Many more, on the other hand, make a hotchpotch of it, and their business ends up looking down-market and unprofessional.

Yes, working with professionals costs money, and may seem unnecessary for a small independent sandwich bar such as your own. You may even think that designing your company logo will be fun. My advice, however, would be to hire a professional, if you can afford it. If you find the right one your initial investment will pay you back ten-fold in the years to come.

You could search for graphic designers on Yell.com and then get in touch with three or four in order to discuss some ideas on a no-obligation basis. Any worth their salt should have a website, or at least be able to post some examples of their work to you. Firms such as Design Remedy (www.designremedy.co.uk) specialize in working with small start-up businesses, and can even take a brief from you over the telephone. You could also consider contacting local art colleges to find out whether any students would be interested in developing your brand as part of a final-year college project.

Ask each designer to quote for a 'getting started' package of work. This would include the development of your sandwich bar logo, your brand colour pallette (two or three pantone colours that you'll use everywhere and on everything), your business card and letter-headed paper. Make sure that you know exactly how many printed copies of your business card and letterhead the quote includes, and that you'll receive the electronic copy of the design files so that you're at liberty to use them and get more copies printed in future. Remember, you're paying for these images to be created, so they don't belong to the designer, they belong to you.

Ensure that you give the designer a concise brief. Remember, their job is to translate the verbal description you provide into a visual image. This is where your business plan will come in handy, as you should have already developed an overview of what your sandwich bar will be like, and the customers you'll try to tempt in. Provide the designer with your key messages; this will help them to understand what it is that you want your logo to convey.

Café Culture

At Taste we're all about fresh, healthier food. So, once we'd developed our brand and key messages, we worked with designremedy.co.uk to make sure that our shop visuals, menus, fascias, website, etc. all communicated a clear, wholesome message about our café. And the result? Within the first few weeks people of the town were already referring to us as 'the fresh place' or 'that healthier café'. The graphic design work was so professional that customers were even asking us if we were part of an established chain. Perfect! Customers know what to expect, and that entices them in.

3
PREPARING TO OPEN

AT A GLANCE

In this chapter we'll cover:

☐ Getting to know the environmental health office

☐ Creating your menu

☐ Sourcing the right suppliers and getting the right price

☐ Fitting out your premises

☐ Establishing your kitchen – hygiene and the law

☐ Managing your kitchen – food preparation and stock control

☐ Health and safety

You've found your premises, you have the money you need to open, you have a business plan you're confident in and a brand that you love. For us this was when our business began to feel real – no longer are you talking about 'if' you open your sandwich bar, but 'when'. Now, even more than before, it will be critical for you to be organized, methodical and maintain your attention to detail.

Getting to know the environmental health office

Having a strong and open relationship with the local environmental health office is invaluable for any sandwich bar owner. In my experience their inspectors are not the scary dragons many people imagine them to be. They are instead professionals, who'll happily work with you to help ensure that the public is not at risk from food poisoning, or worse.

There are some key areas that fall under your local environmental health officer's responsibility.

☐ Food hygiene and safe preparation of food.

☐ Cleaning schedules for the café.

☐ Staff training in food hygiene and safe cleaning.

☐ Pest controls.

☐ Staff personal hygiene.

☐ Health and safety within the shop.

☐ The decorative condition of the shop.

☐ The general working order of equipment within the shop.

At this stage it is beneficial to get in touch with your local enforcement officer, and to strike up a relationship with them. The reason for this is that they can help you to understand food hygiene and health and safety legislation and how it applies to your business. He or she will advise you on the rules relating to how to describe your food on menus and if you should charge VAT. They'll even meet with you at various shop premises you may be considering, and advise of any problems they have spotted from an environmental health point of view. Later, they'll look over your re-fit plans, to ensure that you are including all the required hand-washing facilities, a fan extractor, and clean food preparation areas, etc.

This will greatly reduce the risk of you investing time and money in plans and equipment which later you find are unsuitable and you have to change.

Café Culture

A year ago we were viewing potential premises for our second shop. One unit in particular was a front-runner, because of its high foot-fall location. We asked our local environmental health officer to inspect the premises with us and provide comment. Thank goodness we did. The issues he raised would have meant an additional £10,000 in re-fit costs, something which would have made the unit unviable as a business proposition.

Better to know before you sign on the dotted line, than after.

Forming a relationship early on will also help to demonstrate to your local environmental health officer that you are professional, and that you understand the importance of following government regulations. It certainly doesn't hurt to be in their good books from the start. Remember too that you need to register your new business with your local environmental health office at least 28 days before opening – registration is free.

A great site to visit is the Food Standards Agency (FSA) website (www.food.gov.uk). You can order free of charge publications designed to aid first-time catering business owners, such as:

☐ *FSA – Safer Food, Better Business*

☐ *FSA – A Guide for Business*

☐ *FSA – Health and Safety – a no-nonsense summary of government rules and regulations*

☐ *FSA – Food Law Inspections and Your Business*

Alarm Bell

If you're considering purchasing a going concern then make sure you arrange for the environmental health officer to conduct an inspection. If the seller is not willing to allow such a visit then walk away from the deal. They're hiding something, and if you buy the business you'll end up paying for it in more ways than one.

You can expect an official inspection in your first three months of trading, and then depending on the results of that inspection, at intervals of between six months and a year from then on. Chapter 4 provides tips to ensuring that you are prepared for your first inspection.

Creating your menu

For us, both self-professed foodies; this was one of the most exciting projects to undertake. During the months of research and reconnaissance we'd gathered hundreds of sample menus, made notes of interesting sandwich and salad ideas and collected tonnes of chutney, bread, cheese, cake and sandwich-filling samples. We were also sure of our brand, and what our sandwich bar's image would be. In addition, we'd also worked hard to get under the skin of our target audience, and to understand the kind of food they'd like to see on offer. Armed with all this information we began to formulate our menu.

Throughout this section I'll refer to 'sandwiches'. This does not simply mean the traditional two slices of bread with some filling approach, but the many other variations including the wrap, panini, bagel and baguette. I'm not going to separate the traditional approach from the newer options, as ultimately they are all sandwiches, just served in different bread. I'm also not going to talk about the 'design' of your printed menu, as I'll cover this in Chapter 4. This section is simply about choosing which foods you will (and will not) serve).

FINDING INSPIRATION

You'll already have lots of menus gathered during your initial research, but now you need to cast your net even wider. Supermarkets own magazines are extremely useful, as they're free, and will often suggest seasonal foods and recipes that you could adapt into an idea for a sandwich; Waitrose's publication is particularly good. Also spend time looking through food and cookery magazines such as *BBC Good Food*, and *Olive*, and the trade magazine *Sandwich and Snack News*. Why not look through the recipe books of current chefs such as Gordon Ramsay and Jamie Oliver? Could you turn one of their popular dishes into an idea for a sandwich?

Café Culture

One of the most popular specials we serve is a seafood stick sandwich filling based on a dish Gordon Ramsay cooked up on his F Word TV show in 2007. It's a take on his lime crab starter, and we called it 'Ramsay's Catch'. People loved that they'd watched his TV show, and the next day could buy a sandwich inspired by the same flavours.

WHICH BREAD SHOULD YOU STOCK?

The million-dollar question for any sandwich bar, but unfortunately also one of the most tricky to understand if you are new to the business. The key is to offer the tried and tested alongside the new and exciting. I would suggest that you put yourself in the place of your target customer and ask yourself what they'd prefer? Men generally prefer a bigger bite – thick-sliced bread, baguettes and ciabatta – while women tend to prefer less bread and opt for thinner-sliced breads, wraps and bagels.

OFFERING SOMETHING FOR EVERYONE

The British high street is full of restaurants offering all kinds of world cuisine: Thai, Indian, Chinese, Japanese, Italian, French, Portuguese, Mexican. This must mean that the average sandwich bar customer wants a choice of fillings that continually stimulates his/her palate – right? Wrong.

Café Culture

We currently stock nine choices of bread in our café, and for us this is the optimum balance, as it means that we offer our customers a wide choice, while at the same time we're not left with masses of wastage at the end of the day. White sliced bread is still the most popular choice, with granary and wholemeal sliced coming in a close second. Panini toasties are also incredibly popular. Baguettes, ciabatta, wraps, bagels and thick-sliced crusty bloomer sandwiches all do well, but are sold in lesser degrees. We get the odd request for rye bread, or gluten-free bread, but not enough to convince us that customer demand is high enough for us to introduce them onto our menu.

The truth is that, like the bread you serve, a balance must be struck between innovative new creations and much-loved favourites. You'll have many regulars who like a plain chicken or cheese salad sandwich, and who'll buy the same thing day in, day out. You'll also have a smaller group who like to be excited, and to try the unusual. Your success will come from being able to cater for all, and alienating no one.

Café Culture

At any given time in our sandwich bar we'll have OAPs eating plain cheese white bread sandwiches, office workers tucking into coronation chicken bagels and shoppers devouring hoi sin duck and spring onion wraps. This makes me happy, because I know we're reaching the widest possible target audience, and our business is more secure because of it.

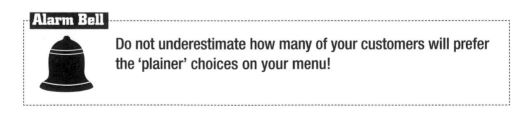

Alarm Bell

Do not underestimate how many of your customers will prefer the 'plainer' choices on your menu!

My advice would be to organize your sandwich filling ideas into three categories. First, 'well-known favourites' such as egg mayo, tuna mayo, cheese and chicken salad. Second, 'familiar favourites' such as minted lamb, seafood cocktail and tandoori chicken. And third, 'unfamiliar newbies', which could be as creative and innovative as you like.

You should aim to keep your menu selection simple and straightforward. If you opt for a pick-and-mix approach, ensure that the formula for working out prices depending on filling and bread type is foolproof and easy to navigate. If you decide to have set sandwich-filling options then ensure that the menu offers customers a wide choice from the three categories outlined above. For this approach I would suggest that one half of the menu comes from the 'well-known favourites' category, just over one quarter comes from the 'familiar favourites' category, and just under one quarter comes from the 'unfamiliar newbies' category.

You should consider introducing a daily or weekly specials board. You'll find that your regular customers welcome it, as it'll help to keep the selection interesting. It's great for you too as it enables you to try out new ideas and gauge interest, and to use up produce that might otherwise go out of date unsold.

Create your database

You'll find it useful if you develop and save your growing menu list on the computer (we used Excel). You'll be able to refer back to the many sandwich ideas you had, even if they don't make it into your original menu. And in the months to come, when you're updating your selection, you'll have a ready-made database to dip into for suggestions.

You could consider setting up various search filters so that you can look for specific sandwich types, or perhaps pick from one of the three categories listed above. We find this invaluable now, and have hundreds of sandwich ideas stored.

MADE TO ORDER OR MADE IN ADVANCE?

During the initial research stage you'll have decided whether your sandwich bar will offer a made-to-order service, or made in advance. However, if you're a first-time reader and you're yet to begin your initial research. I'll explain the difference between the two terms, and give some pointers to help you decide what's best for your sandwich bar.

Made to order:

☐ Traditional sandwich bar approach. The customer explains exactly what they want, and on what bread, and you make it for them.

– Customers like this because they can be as individual and specific as they like, and as they watch you making it they can be sure they're happy with the end result.

– You'll like it because it means you can offer the widest choice of sandwich filling options.

– You may not like it because you have to employ more staff through lunchtime in order to quickly serve the queue of customers.

☐ Made in advance:

– Newer sandwich bar approach, as seen in the like of Pret and EAT. Sandwiches are made early to mid morning, and wrapped/boxed/bagged, then displayed in fridges ready for sale at lunchtime.

– Customers like it because they are in a hurry and may not have time to wait for a sandwich to be made to order.

– You'll like it because you're able to serve lots of customers very quickly at lunchtime.

– You may not like it because you'll have more waste, as unsold sandwiches will have to go in the bin at the end of the day.

So which approach is best for you? Well, that all depends on the kind of sandwich bar you intend to open and the location of your premises. Pret and EAT are shining examples of this 'new' made in advance model. They've created strong brands that customers trust. This means that there's no uncertainty over the freshness of the pre-packed food, as customers are confident that it is as fresh as the companies say it is. Would your brand be so strong? Pret and EAT have also secured prime location, high footfall sites, perfectly geared towards a made in advance approach. Do you think your site will have as high a footfall figure, and that demand for rapid service will be as great?

Only you can decide what's best for your sandwich bar, but in my view as an independent you should concentrate on offering an outstanding made to order service. If, a few months down the line, you're so busy that you are unable to serve your customers fast enough then you can always consider pre-packing a small range of favourite sandwiches for people to 'grab on the run'. Or perhaps introduce a 'pre-order' service, so that people can email or telephone their orders to the shop, and collect straight from the till at lunchtime.

BEYOND THE SANDWICH

You should also be considering other foods to offer on your menu, alongside your sandwich range. This is an excellent idea, as it widens the reach of your net, and attracts even more customers.

Alarm Bell

Don't offer so many foods that customers become confused about what you are and what you sell. Ask yourself; does this fit in with my sandwich bar's image? Also be certain that you can consistently deliver high quality in all these food areas.

It doesn't have to be complicated; in fact, many of your basic sandwich fillings can be altered and tweaked to create something totally different, without much extra effort.

Café Culture

We make a fresh tuna mix, using red onion, garlic and fresh tomato. The great thing is its versatility, as it works well with salad in a sandwich, with cheese in a panini, or hot in a jacket potato.

☐ **Bistro-style meals** – You could offer spaghetti bolognaise or lasagne, perhaps made yourself or bought in from a supplier if you are happy with the quality. The disadvantage is that they do take a while to heat up thoroughly (around eight minutes), which is a lengthy wait for a customer in a sandwich bar. You'd also need to be certain that your trading licence permits you to serve this type of hot food. If you're trading on an A1 licence then it is likely the local planning office would not permit it.

☐ **Soups** – I would wholeheartedly recommend you to add soups to your menu in the winter months as they are an excellent both individual and add-on sale. Depending on your preference, either make the soups at home (using vegetable stock so that they're suitable for vegetarians and meat-eaters alike) or buy from a supplier. The latter is a cost-effective and time-saving approach, and there are many companies that offer excellent quality fresh soups that taste just as good as the homemade variety. Powdered or tinned soup should be avoided if you value your sandwich bar's credibility!

Café Culture

We serve a choice of two soups daily from October through to May. It's an excellent addition to our menu, with many women opting for this instead of a salad, and many men buying soup as well as their usual sandwich.

☐ **Salads** – It's relatively easy to offer an attractive salad selection, using your sandwich bar's existing contents, and some additional mixed leaves such as lollo rosso, radicchio and rocket. You could also consider including delicatessen favourites such as olives, roasted peppers and cold meats.

☐ **Jacket potatoes** – A sandwich bar favourite. They are easy to prepare, customers love them, and they offer excellent profit margins. Please avoid buying in frozen (yes, they do exist!) jacket potatoes. Instead invest in a traditional jacket potato oven, or simply buy a domestic cooker and bake off the potatoes freshly each morning. Your customers will appreciate the difference.

Buy a double domestic oven. That way you can have the lower oven on 200 degrees, cooking potatoes, and the upper oven on 100 degrees keeping cooked potatoes warm ready for sale. It's a much cheaper option than the catering-grade jacket potato oven and warmers available to buy.

☐ **Breakfasts** – Breakfast is naturally a slower time of day; however you can offer a breakfast menu as a way to tempt people in. Consider bacon and sausage sandwiches, toast, and porridge. Office workers are often in a hurry and don't have breakfast at home, which means you could cash in at this time of day.

☐ **Cakes and patisserie** – If you intend your sandwich bar to have a substantial seating area then cakes and patisserie are must have-items. If your sandwich bar will be primarily takeaway then the need is not so great. Either way, opt for freshly sliced cakes if you can, rather than those that are individually foil-packed, and steer away from those containing fresh cream, as this shortens shelf life considerably. You should consider that you'll need fridge space to effectively display your cakes, and that this should not be alongside cold meats etc. Homemade is always preferable to the customer, or you could look for a local baker or patisserie firm that hand makes cakes in small batches for a similar quality.

☐ **Fruit smoothies** – There's been an explosion in fruit smoothie vendors on the high street in the past few years, so much so that they are now almost a 'must-have' menu item for any modern sandwich bar. If you intend to offer smoothies to your customers you have a number of choices. First, you could buy ready-bottled blends, either economy brands from your cash and carry or recognized fresh brands such as Innocent, and stock them alongside other drinks in your grab-and-go fridge. Second, you could buy in pre-packed frozen sachets of fruit, ready to be mixed with fruit juice and blended into a smoothie. Or third, you could create your own imaginative blends using fresh fruit, juices and ice. Your choice will depend on your sandwich bar, and your customer's expectations.

 Take a trip to your local smoothie bar, and you'll see that they use frozen fruit to make their smoothies. This is because frozen fruit has its goodness locked in, and its shelf life is far longer.

☐ **Fruit** – All good-quality sandwich bars have a fresh fruit basket alongside the till for customers to pick from. Fruit makes an excellent add-on sale, as it's healthy and relatively low in price (but you can still make a good margin). Granny Smith's, Red Delicious and bananas are popular. Make sure the fruit is washed and clean and always looking its best. If you've fridge space you could also consider selling pre-packed fruit salads. In a sealed tub they'll only keep for two days, so there is a risk of wastage, however, in the summer months sales should be brisk. Either make these yourself using a combination of grapes, melon, pineapple, strawberry, etc. or perhaps ask your local greengrocer if they can source some ready packed for you.

THE COFFEE CONNECTION

Virtually everyone who sits down to eat in your sandwich bar will also buy a cup of coffee or tea. The same will apply to your takeaway breakfast customers, and to many of those people taking away food at lunchtime. Hot drinks will play a massive part in your day, and so should be considered seriously on your menu.

Will you offer basic, good-quality filter coffee, or will you offer a wider choice of freshly prepared Italian lattes, cappuccinos, machiattos, and mochas? Will you offer a simple breakfast tea, or will you also offer Earl Grey, Ceylon, Green, White, Liquorice, Berry and Camomile? Don't underestimate how important having the right hot drink offering is. Spend time sourcing the best-quality coffee and tea, and ensure that you receive training on how to use the equipment you decide to install in your café. Many suppliers can provide the coffee beans, the various tea blends, as well as the flavoured syrups and powders to create individual drinks. In addition they'll provide the coffee machine, tea urn, water boiler, etc. that you need to get started.

 **If you decide to sell a range of premium coffees such as lattes and cappuccinos then you should also ensure that your menu offers simple white or black coffee too. There will always be people who are either not interested in or confused by the various choices of coffee, and if you don't want to alienate them your menu needs to have what we like to call a 'safe haven' option for them to choose from.**

SPECIALIST FOOD

No matter what kind of sandwich bar you intend to open, these days it's vital that you have at least a basic understanding of the various 'specialist' food requirements of customers.

Organic

Demand for organic food has increased drastically over the past few years, but unfortunately it is still not mainstream enough to be cost-effective, and has to be sourced from a specialist supplier. The high price point is a turn-off for many customers, and this is the reason we don't have an organic food offering in our café. However, that's not to say organic food won't be right for your sandwich bar.

If you do decide to sell organic, beware! The word 'organic' is one that is strictly defined by law, and may only be used by producers and manufacturers who are registered with a recognized organic accreditation organization. In order to become registered, members must:

☐ Follow a strict set of guidelines laid down by national and international law.

☐ Keep thorough and accurate records of production processes.

☐ Submit to annual and random inspections.

You will need to ensure that the produce you say is organic is certified organic. This can be a costly and lengthy process, and one that is probably only worthwhile if your entire sandwich bar offering is based on the premise that you are 'all organic'.

The Organic Food Federation (www.orgfoodfed.com) and the Soil Association (www.soilassociation.org.uk) are just two organizations that provide accreditation schemes. If you are considering selling a high proportion of organic food, and wish to become accredited, I suggest you contact the British Sandwich Association for advice (www.sandwich.org.uk).

Café Culture

A significant proportion of our customers are Muslim, and for this reason we chose to use entirely halal chicken for our fillings and mixes.

Choosing to serve halal chicken makes good business sense. Both Muslims and non-Muslims can eat halal, so this ensures you can serve the widest possible audience.

Halal

This is the meat eaten by Muslims. The word 'halal' literally means permissible, and in translation it is usually used as lawful. The Halal Food Authority rules for halal are based on Islamic Shari'ah, and they govern the way that meat is slaughtered. For non-Muslims, eating halal meat simply means that they can be confident the animal has been slaughtered in a humane way.

It is relatively easy to source halal meat, particularly chicken. You should ask your supplier for a copy of their halal accreditation certificate, and check the details thoroughly. You should also be aware that practising Muslims do not eat pork, or any food that may have come into contact with pork. For more information visit The Halal Food Authority's website (www.halafoodauthority. co.uk).

Kosher

Kosher is the Jewish way of eating, and central to it are certain strict laws governing what can and cannot be consumed. According to the laws of the Torah, the only types of meat that may be eaten are cattle and game that have 'cloven hooves' and 'chew the cud'. If an animal species fulfils only one of these conditions (for example the pig, which has split hooves but does not chew the cud or the camel, which chews the cud but does not have split hooves), then its meat may not be eaten.

Similarly to halal meat, to be eaten, a kosher species must be slaughtered by a ritual slaughterer, and since Jewish law prohibits causing any pain to animals, the slaughtering has to be effected in such a way that unconsciousness is instantaneous and death occurs almost instantaneously.

If you are intending on selling kosher produce you will need to ensure that it is accredited by a recognized scheme. For more information about worldwide accreditation schemes visit www.badatz.org.

Vegetarian

The official term for a vegetarian is someone who eats a diet of grains, pulses, nuts, seeds, vegetables and fruits, with or without the use of dairy products and eggs. A vegetarian does not eat any meat, poultry, game, fish, shellfish or crustacea, or slaughter by-products.

You'll probably find that a significant proportion of your customer base is vegetarian, or perhaps if not a 'true' vegetarian then certainly looking for ways to reduce the amount of meat they eat. It's definitely worthwhile offering a varied choice of vegetarian sandwich options, beyond cheese salad!

 You should ensure that about 15–20% of the sandwich fillings available are suitable for vegetarians.

The Vegetarian Society website has a section dedicated to businesses with vegetarian customers, and you'll find guidance and recipe ideas (www.vegsoc.org).

Vegan

A vegan diet is one free from any animal produce. This means no meat, shellfish, cheese, milk, honey or butter. Fruits, vegetables, grains, nuts, seeds, legumes (beans, lentils and split peas) and fungi (mushrooms, yeasts), and food made from these are on the menu, however.

The Vegan Society website is an excellent source of information, and their guidebook *Vegan – Catering for All* offers hints, tips and recipes for chefs and caterers. Visit www.vegansociety.com.

Intolerant

Many people suffer from food intolerances. This means that they have an adverse (although not life-threatening) reaction when they eat certain foods, or types of foods. Some of the most common food intolerances are to dairy (lactose intolerance) and gluten (coeliac disease).

As the owner of a sandwich bar you should ensure that you have a basic understanding of food intolerances, so that you can ensure customers requesting a lunch 'free' from a particular type of food are served correctly. The Food Standards Agency website (www.eatwell.gov.uk) is helpful, as is the BBC website (www.bbc.co.uk/health).

Allergic

Unlike intolerances, food allergies can be potentially life-threatening, and you must ensure that you are aware of the risks posed to customers in your sandwich bar. If you make your sandwiches freshly to order then it is the responsibility of the customer to check whether any of the ingredients they are allergic to are contained in the sandwich they have ordered. However, if you pre-pack any of your sandwiches then you must ensure your labels contain an allergy alert, for example 'this product contains nuts'.

For more information, visitwww.allergyuk.org, the website of the medical charity for people with allergies, to help you understand the nature of allergies, and also www.eatwell.gov.uk.

It is sensible to discuss specialist food issues such as these, with your local food hygiene inspector, as they will be able to recommend suitable reading, training and provide up-to-date advice.

TOP TIP

You're not expected to know everything about food intolerances and allergies, but you are expected to be prepared should a customer request confirmation that something you're serving them is OK for them to eat. Just be honest. If you're not sure, double-check the ingredients for them. If the ingredients list in inconclusive, tell them as much. They need to be able to make an informed decision. Don't be tempted to say it's OK if you're not certain.

SERVING AND PACKAGING YOUR FOOD

You've spent a huge amount of time considering the food and drink you'll serve in your sandwich bar. Now you need to spend some time considering how you'll serve it. Will you use cups and saucers or mugs for your coffee? Will you serve your sandwiches on china plates when customers sit down for lunch, or simply wrapped in greaseproof paper? Will you invest in ripple-wrap heat-resistant takeaway cups for hot drinks, or opt for the cheaper paper variety? Will your takeaway packaging be branded, or plain? Let's consider the issues one at a time.

Takeaway

Takeaway food plays a huge part in any sandwich bar's business, so having the right packaging is critical. There's a wide range to choose from, but the basics that most sandwich bars will need are as follows:

☐ **Drinks cups and lids**. Varying in size, and perhaps with heat-resistant grips, so customers don't burn their hands. We opted to sell two sizes of coffee (regular and large), rather than three sizes (small, medium and large). This saves on packaging costs, as we only need to buy and store two sizes of cup. Our customers are perfectly happy with this choice – in fact, many say they prefer it to the multitude of choices they face in big-name coffee shops. We also opted for 'ripple-wrap' cups, as they have the heat shield built in.

☐ **Sandwich packaging**. If you intend to make sandwiches to order then you'll simply require greaseproof paper (to wrap the sandwich in) and a paper bag (to put the sandwich in). However, if you are intending to pre-make packed sandwiches then you'll be faced with a wide choice of boxes, bags and other containers you could display them in. When deciding which boxes suit your business consider how easy they are to use (i.e. will a member of staff find packing sandwiches quick and easy, or time-consuming and fiddly?), the cost per box, and also whether the box style suits your brand image.

☐ **Food boxes**. If you are planning to serve food such as jacket potatoes, salads and pastas then you'll need a heat-resistant box to sell them in. Consider their various uses: are they flexible enough to enable customers to add a small side salad? Can they be heated in the microwave? Do they fit with your brand image?

☐ **Various**. Don't forget the many other smaller items of packaging you'll need for takeaway food service, for example plastic cutlery, napkins, carrier bags, smoothie/milkshake cups and lids.

There are many suppliers offering takeaway packing to sandwich bars. What should you consider when choosing the right one for you?

☐ **Packaging range**. The packaging you choose should make your food look its most beautiful and appetizing; it should also fit perfectly with your brand image, and be easy to use, efficient to store and cost-effective. Request as may samples as you need from suppliers, and try them out at home before you decide.

☐ **Minimum order**. Many suppliers have a high minimum order threshold. This means that you'll need plenty of space to store takeaway packaging, or else deep pockets to pay delivery charges. Discuss this with the supplier; they may be willing to negotiate the minimum order level in order to secure your business.

☐ **Delivery days**. How quickly can a supplier replenish your stocks? Ideally you should be able to receive a delivery one or two days after you place the order. Any longer and you run the risk of being left high and dry.

☐ **Suppliers**. Firms you should look into include Tri-Star, Planglow and Sovereign.

To keep cost and storage to a minimum try to think of different ways in which the packaging that you choose could be used. For example, could you use the takeaway coffee cups for soup in the winter, rather than buying in specialist soup containers?

Café Culture

Branded takeaway packaging looks great, and there's a lot to be said for the job it does in promoting your café's name. The unfortunate truth is, though, that it is expensive, and out of reach for many sandwich bars. This is not necessarily because of the cost of design and printing (although this is costly), but because of the massive quantities of packaging you then need to buy in.

We decided that we'd get stickers printed instead of having our packaging branded. Now, we stick our stickers on our coffee cups and jacket potato boxes, which gives the branded look but at a fraction of the cost. It does take a little time, but to be honest it's the ideal ten-minute job for our staff to do at 11.30am, once the café is set for lunch and we're awaiting the rush to start. We don't sticker everything all in one go, we just make sure that we've enough packaging to see us through the next few days, and keep refreshing stocks when they get low.

Eat in

If you are intending to serve customers eating in your café then you may feel you'd prefer to offer an alternative to paper takeaway cups, etc. Certainly if you have any more than two tables you should consider offering your customers formal plates and cups.

- ☐ **Drinks**. You need to decide whether you'll serve hot drinks in a cup and saucer or a mug, and whether you'll serve tea directly in the cup or provide the customer with a teapot. Consider the style of your café, and the speed of service. Will you have time during a busy lunch to fill little individual teapots, provide little jugs of milk, etc. or would it be more time efficient to serve tea directly in stylish mugs? You also need to think about whether you'll have one central condiment and napkin station, or if you'll have condiment and napkins on each table.

- ☐ **Food**. If you're plating sandwiches you should take time to consider how they'll be sliced and served. Will you provide a small salad garnish, or perhaps a couple of crisps? Also consider other foods that you serve, such as jacket potatoes, soup and cakes. Will they require a different type of plate or bowl? Remember cutlery; perhaps consider using metal knives and forks for customers eating in.

- ☐ **Quality**. The cups, plates and bowls that you choose will need to be incredibly hard wearing, as they'll be in constant use, and suffer many knocks along the way. For this reason you should invest in catering-grade items that are easily replaceable. Catering supplier Nisbets has an excellent low-cost range.

It is often very cost-effective to buy china branded with your café logo. Firms such as Quickfire Tableware (www.coffeecups.co.uk) have many low-cost but hard-wearing modern ranges, all of which can be branded. If you're starting out, and are buying everything from scratch, it's certainly worth considering.

Sourcing suppliers and getting the right price

You'll have realized a few months back, while undertaking your research, that there are literally thousands of suppliers in the sandwich bar marketplace.

During your trade show visits you'll have collected many brochures and product lists, and you'll have made notes of which products are stocked by the many sandwich bars you've visited. Now you need to start distilling down this information, creating a list of suppliers that could provide you with the products you need, at the right price.

Café Culture

We use 15 different suppliers, who provide us with everything from our fresh bread to our toilet rolls. Over the past three years we've changed some of them, but most we're happy with and have been using from the start. I'm so glad that I spent time thoroughly researching the suppliers available to us before we opened. As a busy café owner I know I would now struggle to find the time to revisit this lengthy process again.

CREATING YOUR SHOPPING LIST

First you need to create your shopping list. This should, of course, be based on the draft menu you've created, but will also include items that would not appear on your menu, such as snacks, store cupboard ingredients and cleaning materials. Let's consider the kinds of foods and produce you could require:

☐ **Breads** – Traditional white, wholemeal and granary sliced breads, rolls and baguettes. Crusty bloomer breads, Italian ciabatta and focaccia, gluten-free bread, pitta bread, organic loaves, rye bread, deep-fill baps and subs, flat breads, stone-baked breads, walnut loaves, etc.

☐ **Cakes** – Carrot cake, banana loaf, chocolate cake, Victoria sandwich, teacakes, scones, muffins, biscotti, cookies, tray bakes, flapjacks, brownies, etc.

☐ **Store cupboard staples** – Sauces, jams, marmalades, dressings, marinades, mustards, mayonnaises, pickles, dry herbs.

☐ **Delicatessen produce** – Cold meats, cheeses, eggs, seafood, coleslaw, potato salad, olives, sun-dried tomatoes, minted lamb mix, coronation chicken mix, tuna mayo mix.

☐ **Fruit and veg** – Lettuce, tomato, cucumber, onion, apples, bananas, grapes, fresh herbs, baking potatoes, strawberries.

☐ **Milk** – Full-fat, semi and skimmed, cream, soya, goat's milk.

□ **Packaging** – takeaway coffee cups and lids, straws, greaseproof paper, takeaway carrier bags, napkins.

□ **Drinks** – Tea, coffee, hot chocolate, herbal teas, frappe, chai, iced tea, decaffeinated coffee.

□ **Snacks** – Crisps, rice cakes, seeds, nuts, dried fruit, chocolate, organic chocolate, canned drinks, bottled water, bottled juices, cartons.

□ **Hygiene** – Latex gloves, antibacterial spray, cleaning gels and liquids, hand-wash and paper towels, mop heads.

CONTACTING SUPPLIERS

Next, you need to begin contacting a range of suppliers and requesting free samples, and price lists. Don't just stick to one type of supplier; mix it up a little with national firms, smaller regional specialists, and local independents.

Suppliers will naturally be very keen to talk to you. Take advantage of this, ask to visit their premises, seek advice on what new trends in food and drink are increasingly popular, and find out if they offer any free training. You should also ask them the following questions:

□ How often they make deliveries to your area, and on what days.

□ What time they make the deliveries (early deliveries may demand that the driver has a key, and you won't want deliveries between 12 and 2pm).

□ How orders should be placed (many have a set day of the week for ordering, and the sales team will call you at an agreed time from a call list).

□ Whether there is a minimum order level (some order levels can be prohibitively high).

□ Whether you'll be able to set up an account (it's a far better way for you to manage cash flow).

□ Whether they supply any other sandwich bars or cafés in the area (it's better to stock produce that is unique to your locality).

□ Whether deliveries are made in temperature-controlled vans (they must be, if the goods are perishable).

□ If they'll negotiate on price. As a general rule you should be able to negotiate some discount from the list price. After all, you're giving them regular business, and they want to sign you up as a new account.

Don't be afraid to ask for free samples. In the months before we opened we requested so many breads, meats, cheeses, sandwich mixes, etc. that our weekly supermarket bill was virtually non-existent!

PRICE CHECKING

Next, begin to price check the food and produce the suppliers are offering. Your aim is to find out whether the price you'll buy the produce at will enable you to make the profit levels your business plan requires.

This activity is not an exact science, especially at this stage of the process when you're yet to open, and your calculations are based on estimates. However, it's vital that you do these sums – after all, there's no point in deciding to use a particular supplier and then three months in you realize that you're paying way more than you can afford for the produce. Here are some pointers:

□ Decide on 'set' portions for sandwich, baguette, bagel, jacket potato fillings, etc. For example, you could decide that your sliced bread sandwiches will all contain two tablespoons of filling.

□ Calculate the weight of these set portions. For example, two tablespoons of egg mayo could weigh around 90g. Do this by weighing some of the samples you've received.

□ Develop a comprehensive list (we used an Excel spreadsheet) of the suppliers you are considering for each produce item. List the weight they sell the produce in, and how much that weight would cost you.

□ From these figures you'll be able to calculate how much each supplier's filling will cost you to sell as an individual sandwich. For example, if a supplier sells their egg mayo filling in 1kg tubs, and you use 90g of filling per sandwich, then you'll get 11 sandwiches out of each tub. If they price 1kg of egg mayo filling at £4.30 then you'll know that each sandwich will require 39p worth of filling.

□ Now add in the cost of two slices of bread, and a set figure for additional salad stuffs such as lettuce and tomato, plus greaseproof paper, napkins, takeaway bags, and you'll have a good idea of how much each of your menu items will cost you to make.

☐ Compare the total cost of producing the food item with the price you intend to sell it for. Are you left with a 65% margin? If not, then you should perhaps look for an alternative supplier for the produce, or reconsider your menu.

To be thorough you need to repeat this exercise for everything you intend to produce and sell. It is absolutely vital that you know exactly how much each item costs you, and that you make the right level of profit from its sale.

Café Culture

We had created our draft menu and were really happy with it. One star sandwich was set to be an Italian inspired mix of Parma ham, mozzarella cheese and handmade tomato chutney. However, on doing our cost calculations we soon realized that Parma ham was simply too expensive, and that we'd have to price the sandwich so high that customers in our local area would consider it too expensive. We took the decision to make the sandwich with traditional ham instead, and amended our menu before it was printed. Our customers love the sandwich and it's always been one of our most popular, plus we make a healthy profit on every one we sell.

Alarm Bell

Remember, it's not simply about getting the lowest price. You need a supplier that can provide you with the quality of produce you want, for the price that suits your bottom line, and with a reliable service.

The suppliers you choose are important because their reliability, and the safety and quality of the food they supply, could affect your own business. It's especially important that the products you buy have been stored, processed and handled safely.

ESTABLISH SUPPLY AND DELIVERY PROCEDURES

Finally, before your café opens and you begin receiving your first deliveries, you need to do the following:

☐ Create a list, to be mounted on the wall in easy view, of all the suppliers you'll be using, their order days, delivery days, and contact telephone numbers.

Alarm Bell

Traceability is all-important. You must keep written records of all of the suppliers that provide you with food, or food ingredients. The records should include the name and address of the supplier, the type and quantity of products and dates when you take delivery. You may also choose to record the batch number or the 'use by' or 'best before' date. Often this information can be found on the invoice or delivery note, but you should double-check to make sure.

You must also keep the invoices and receipts for all the food products you buy from any supplier, including food you've purchased at the local supermarket or cash and carry. This is so that if there is a problem with the food you've sold, you or an enforcement officer can check the information relating to it.

☐ Buy a clipboard and develop your own template order sheet for each supplier. This should list the produce you have decided to source from each supplier. Every time you place an order, fill in a new sheet, ticking the boxes next to each produce item, and noting the expected delivery day. Then keep the sheet on the clipboard until the delivery arrives and has been checked off against the list. This is a particularly useful system if you're working with a partner, as each of you can see who's ordered what and when it is expected in, avoiding confusion.

☐ Send a letter to all your chosen suppliers asking them to confirm in writing that their business complies with all relevant food hygiene regulations and that they have in place an appropriate system of Hazard Analysis Critical Control Point (HACCP). (See Chapter 4 for more information on this.) This is simply a way to ensure that they are working within the law, and the environmental health officer would applaud your professionalism. In addition, such letters may well prove helpful in the unlikely event of a claim being made against you.

☐ Have a clear 'delivery' procedure, so that all staff know what do when a delivery arrives. You should use a thermometer to check that chilled and frozen food is cold enough. You should check that packaging is not damaged, that the 'use by' date is acceptable, and finally, that it's what you ordered.

Fitting out your premises

Fitting out your premises is not simply about painting a few walls and buying and installing equipment (although that will play a big part). By the end of the fit-out process you should have a sandwich bar that;

- ☐ Conforms to hygiene and health and safety standards.

- ☐ Visually appeals to your target customers.

- ☐ Has a clever mix of fixtures and fittings.

- ☐ Has suitable and easy to maintain equipment.

- ☐ Provides you with a practical and efficient working environment.

COMPLYING WITH HYGIENE STANDARDS

As a sandwich bar your business must, first and foremost, comply with hygiene rules concerning the production and sale of food. In a nutshell this means that your premises must be well maintained and clean, and must allow you to follow good food hygiene practices, including protection against contamination and, in particular, pest control.

 **When developing your design scheme it's a good idea to ask your local authority health inspector for advice. You should do this as early as possible, even before you begin agreeing the Heads of Terms. You need them to be on your side.**

It's important to bear in mind the many hygiene rules concerning the design and layout of your sandwich bar, for example:

- ☐ **Hand-washing facilities** – You must have enough washbasins for staff to wash their hands, with hot and cold running water, and materials for cleaning hands and drying them hygienically. You must have separate sinks for hand-washing and washing food produce. Hygiene inspectors prefer you to have a dedicated hand-wash sink located in your food prep area, rather than just using the one in the WC.

- ☐ **Floors and walls** – The rules state that floors and walls should be in 'sound condition', and easy to clean and disinfect. In practice this means that they should be of a smooth and washable material. Tiles are an excellent choice. Washable paint is a cheaper alternative.

☐ **Ceilings** – Should be constructed in a way that prevents dirt building up, with no flaking paint, etc. You should also consider that any light fixtures hanging over a food prep area should be enclosed, to prevent a broken bulb dropping shards of glass and contaminating work surfaces.

☐ **Surfaces** – Should be easy to maintain and disinfect. A laminated kitchen work surface is sufficient, although stainless steel is the most hard-wearing and hygienic. Beware if you're considering a natural wooden surface, as it may not be able to cope with the continual daily use, and become porous, and thus unhygienic.

☐ **Shop layout** – Toilets must not lead directly on to food prep areas, cleaning equipment must be stored away from food prep areas, rubbish must be collected away from food prep areas.

Café Culture

We didn't leave the layout to chance. Instead we bought rolls of masking tape and mapped out equipment and furniture on the concrete floor of the empty shop unit. We walked around the mapped-out space, deciding whether the flow of customers through the shop would be smooth, whether we'd be able to work efficiently and have enough room for storage. It was one of the most worthwhile exercises we undertook!

PROVIDING TOILET FACILITIES

Planning regulations are becoming far stricter when it comes to cafés providing toilet facilities to their customers. Many councils are now stipulating that new cafés *must* provide toilet facilities (often as a way for them to pass on the financial burden of providing municipal public toilets). Before you open you should speak to the planning office at your local authority and find out what toilet provision you will be required to make. You should consider that you might be required to provide disabled toilet facilities too.

I happen to know that Pret A Manger and Starbucks frequently don't provide toilet facilities for their customers, so there are planning regulation loopholes that enable new cafés to open without a customer toilet facility. If you find that your local planning office is stipulating that you must install toilet facilities, and yet a few shops down the road there is a café such as Starbucks that has not, use it as an example and ask why.

Whether or not you want to provide toilets is ultimately down to personal preference. Because I know that there are clean public toilets close by my sandwich bar I am happy that we do not allow customers to use our toilet, and that it is reserved for staff use only. However, if your café is perhaps located on a small high street, with no local convenience, and if you have a reasonably sized eat-in area, you may feel obliged to allow customers to use your facilities.

My advice would be as follows. Do not advertise your toilet (with a WC sign on the door). If you do then passers-by will notice it and soon everyone from passing school children to those waiting for the bus will begin to use it as their local toilet stop (without spending any money). Put a notice up in the toilet explaining that this is a staff toilet, and requesting that customers please leave it as clean and tidy as they find it. Check it once every hour or so, to ensure it is clean.

Café Culture

Our café is located within a private shopping mall, and we are tenants of the mall. The mall, like most like it, provides extensive customer toilet and baby-changing facilities. Because of this we are thankfully not obliged to provide our customers with toilet facilities. This may sound rather jaded, but having seen the mess customers make just drinking a cup of coffee, I dread to think of the mess I'd face having to clean up after them in the toilet. Aside from this, providing customer toilets does mean a strain on the workload, as staff need to be assigned the responsibility of cleaning them throughout the day.

A PSYCHOLOGICAL APPROACH

Here comes the science bit . . . Consider the following motivational factors – budget, convenience, health, indulgence, lifestyle, conscience, nostalgia, hygiene. All of these evoke a powerful psychological response in food retail customers.

Now take a look at how the big food chains satisfy these motivators, and entice customers in. Marks & Spencer's newly refurbished stores are a shining example, as are most Pret cafés, and restaurants in the Strada and Prezzo chains. You'll see that they all have something in common. They use key visual anchors, clues to the style, content and attitude of their business, to help customers feel reassured that they'll find what they're looking for and that their needs will be met.

There's no reason why you can't employ this same psychology when designing your own sandwich bar. For example, stainless steel denotes cleanliness and quality. Consider using this somewhere customers will see it. Perhaps consider using handwritten black boards, as they subconsciously tell people that your food is homemade and wholesome. If you want to make people feel nostalgic for traditional foods, then maybe consider modelling your design scheme on an old-fashioned butchers, with brick-shaped tiles and plenty of scrubbed wooden surfaces.

Alarm Bell

Remember your brand! Throughout your fit-out you need to keep your sandwich bar's brand at the forefront of your mind. Paint colours should mirror those used on business cards, letterheads and shop signs, while fixtures and fittings should be in keeping with your theme.

DECIDING ON FIXTURES AND FITTINGS

Chairs, tables, mirrors, pictures, lighting, flooring, window-dressing, baskets, plants – all are expensive. The key is to achieve a polished and thought-through look, while keeping the budget to a minimum. Like everything, you'll find this is a balancing act. On the one hand you need to ensure you get good value for money, but on the other hand you can't scrimp on quality because the everyday wear and tear will soon take its toll.

Don't overlook lighting!

Why? Because lighting is probably the single most important thing in retail design, particularly in the retailing of food. Choose the wrong colour or brightness of bulb and you make your beautiful fresh display look out of date and unappetizing. Get it right and everything comes to life, looking fresh, natural and appealing.

Where you can, opt for bright halogen bulbs, targeted directly at food produce. Also try and use the newer 'natural' light bulbs, which give off a clean and sunlit quality of light. Your electrician or your local lighting shop will be able to advise you.

Tables, chairs and stools

The mixture of seating you opt for really does depend on the style of café you are creating. Consider your business plan. Are you going to be targeting shoppers and mums? They'll want more comfortable seating; with space to park pushchairs. Are you targeting office workers, being primarily a takeaway? You'll need only to make room for a few small groups of tables, and perhaps some bar-style seating.

When choosing your style of seating consider your brand image. Nostalgic and traditional cafés should perhaps consider second-hand furniture, rustic and individual, while hi-tec, modern sandwich bars could opt for a more utilitarian look with plenty of stainless steel.

Alarm Bell

Always make sure that you consider your responsibility to the public. Whatever seating you provide needs to be safe and sturdy.

It's tempting, when working to a tight budget, to pick up furniture from stores such as IKEA. This is an OK quick fix, but the build quality is simply not up to the level of wear and tear experienced through everyday café use. Ideally you should source furniture from specialist catering furniture suppliers such as Nisbets, Furniture@Work and Café Reality.

Floor coverings

This will be one of your biggest expenses in terms of decorating your sandwich bar. It'll also be something you'd prefer not to have to re-do anytime soon, as it's a massive task to remove all the equipment to re-lay floor surfaces once the shop is up and running. For these reasons you are best to opt for commercial-grade products, and have them fitted professionally. This way they'll stand the test of time, and many thousands of feet!

To get some ideas for possible floor coverings take a trip down your local high street, and see what the big stores use. Heavy-duty laminates in wood and stone effect seem to be particularly popular at the moment. The advantage with laminates is that you can ask the fitter to continue them up the wall, to a skirting board height, thus ensuring more effecting mopping and cleaning.

 If your budget is tight perhaps consider using more of your money on an expensive fashionable floor covering in the customer area, and a lower cost, less stylish one in the kitchen area.

Alarm Bell

 The floor covering you choose will need to be non-slip and easy to hygienically clean, or the hygiene inspector won't be happy!

Alarm Bell

 If you plan on playing background music in your café then you'll need to obtain a licence, and pay a small annual fee. Visit www.mcps-prs-alliance.co.uk to find out more.

CHOOSING THE RIGHT EQUIPMENT

Starting a sandwich bar from scratch means that you'll have to buy absolutely everything you need to equip your café. This is a gargantuan task, but one that does have its advantages.

Think of it as building your own home. You can specify exactly what you want, and create a working environment that suits your café's needs perfectly. Let's consider the various pieces of equipment that you'll need: serve-over display counter, kitchen fridges and freezers, grab-and-go fridge, contact grill and hot water boiler; soup kettle, prep benches, blender, oven, fly killer, extractor/heating/air conditioning unit; microwave, till, toasters.

Serve-over display counter

If you're opting for a traditional, made-to-order sandwich bar model then the serve-over counter is absolutely central to your operation. It will be the centrepiece of your shop.

As a general rule this type of equipment should be bought new. This guarantees that for the first year at least, you'll have it fixed quickly and without hassle should anything go wrong. As the centrepiece of your shop, where the vast majority of your business is conducted, this back-up is all-important.

You'll be able to choose from a wide range of style and size, and what you opt for really depends on your own requirements. However, bear in mind that two smaller units may offer you more future flexibility than one large one. In addition, two smaller units will give you the opportunity to separate certain foods, such as sandwich fillings and cakes, something the hygiene inspector will approve of, as it limits the risk of contamination.

Kitchen fridges and freezers

You'll be faced with a number of choices over size, shape, build quality, commercial, domestic, new, second hand, and so on. What you should do is assess each of your refrigerated and frozen storage requirements individually before making a decision.

For example, you'll have one or two main fridges and freezers in your kitchen. The fridges will store your packs of meat, packs of cheeses, tubs of sandwich fillings, salad stuffs, opened chutneys and pickles, etc. The freezers will store frozen sausages, prawns and breads such as panini and ciabatta. In my experience you should always buy new, commercial appliances for this purpose. They'll be working extra hard, being opened and closed hundreds of times per week, taking the weight of catering-size tubs and packs of foodstuffs, and being generally bashed about a bit. If they break you're entire food stock could be lost, so you need to invest in the best quality you can, and have them regularly serviced. You should choose fridges and freezers that have external digital temperature displays so that you can constantly ensure that they are functioning in the safe temperature zone.

Alarm Bell

Make sure you schedule in a monthly 'condenser clean' for each of your fridges and freezers. The condensers suck in air, and with it lots of dust, so they can get clogged up. If this happens they overheat and break down, costing about £150 to be fixed. It's simple to use either a stiff brush, or toothbrush, to sweep out the dirt, and keep your equipment running smoothly.

In addition to these main fridges and freezers you may have a requirement for smaller, secondary appliances for other foodstuffs. For example, a smaller freezer could be located in your customer service area, to store small quantities of frozen smoothie blends and ice cream ready for quick preparation of customer drink orders. Or a small fridge, in which you might store milk for preparing lattes and cappuccinos. In this instance, as long as the units are intended to be out of customer view, you could consider second-hand domestic models, as their use will be less intensive, and if they break down it won't impact on your ability to operate your business.

Consider buying all your refrigeration and freezer equipment from one supplier, and negotiate a significant discount.

Grab-and-go fridge

Otherwise known as a dairy unit or an open-fronted display chiller, this is where you'll store your drinks, and perhaps some pre-packed sandwiches and salad bowls, plus chocolate in the summer months. They are very cleverly designed so that they stay refrigerated even though they are open to the front, making them perfect for retailing produce for the customer in a hurry, as they can literally 'grab and go'.

As this unit, like your serve-over counter, will be central to your food retailing, it is important to choose one that looks modern, clean and is of high quality. For most made-to-order style sandwich bars a unit 1–1.5 metres wide should be sufficient. However, if your business will offer primarily pre-made sandwiches then you'll need to consider having much more grab-and-go display space for your sandwich boxes, etc.

Café Culture

Because chilled drinks are not 'critical' to our business's ability to operate and make money, we took the decision to buy a second-hand grab-and-go fridge, and paid about £800 for a stainless steel Arneg machine (new costs around £2,500). Because of the simplicity of the motor, there's not an awful lot that can go wrong with refrigeration, and since buying it we've spent approximately £300 on a new motor, and a new fan. Buying second-hand in this case has paid off massively for us.

Coffee machine

As I mentioned in Chapter 2, there are various types of coffee machine, and many decisions you'll need to make. Will you choose a manual or an automatic machine? Will you require one, two, or three steam arms? One, two, or three heads? The decision you make will very much depend on how big a role coffee will play in your business.

Try and ensure that your entire range of customer facing equipment is made of the same material and finish, as it makes your shop look smart and professional. For example, if your coffee machine is stainless steel, try and choose a grab-and-go fridge and serve-over counters with at least an element of stainless steel in their finish. It does not matter so much in your kitchen!

If one of your primary goals is to sell coffee, and your business is going to be positioned as a coffee shop, then it's definitely worth investing in a good coffee machine. You should also opt for the manual approach, rather than automatic. After all, you're an independent café, and a big part of the appeal to customers is the care and attention you show in the preparation of food and drink.

As I mentioned earlier, don't be tempted to buy a second-hand machine. Yes, the investment in a new machine is one of the biggest you'll make, but it'll be worth it. If you buy a second-hand machine you'll never be certain of its condition, and how much life it has left. If it breaks down your business will grind to a halt, and you'll have an expensive engineer's bill to cope with.

When making your decision take a look back at your business plan and cash flow forecasts. How many customers do you expect to purchase coffee per day? Do you anticipate that this will be spread evenly throughout the day, or will all of the sales come in one breakneck two-hour lunch rush?

Now visit some coffee shops – Costa, Starbucks, Caffé Nero, and of course some independents. Which machines do they use? How many steam arms are used to steam the milk? How many coffee heads do the machines have? How many staff do they have making coffee? How many customers do they serve per hour?

How does this compare to your own estimations? Armed with this information you'll begin to develop a clearer picture of the kind of machine your own business will require.

While you're visiting other coffee shops, start to consider how you want to position your coffee machine. Facing the customers, or with its back to the customers? We chose to have the back of the coffee machine facing the customer, so you can chat while making their drink. This works for us for two reasons. First, one member of staff can serve at the till and make coffee at the same time, as they're facing the customers, rather than standing with their back to them. This reduces the wage bill. Second, it meant that we didn't need to invest in an expensive designer machine, as customers see only its stainless steel back, and this kept our initial budget down.

Contact grill

Otherwise known as a panini grill, or sandwich toaster. You could use a contact grill for two purposes. First, it can be used for cooking hot sausages and bacon to order for sandwiches. As both the top and bottom plates heat up it means the meat cooks very quickly and so enables you to offer a cooked-to-order service, which many customers like. Just be aware that it can get a little messy and so this should be a job you will carry out in your kitchen. Your meat-cooking grill should also be dedicated to cooking meat, and not double up as a sandwich toaster.

For meat cooking you should look for a contact grill with a griddle surface and tilted plates (like a lean mean grilling machine). This will allow for the fat produced in the cooking process to drip and be collected safely, rather than building up on flat plates. We have found that good-quality domestic griddle contact grills are perfectly suited to this task. As mentioned in Chapter 2, they cost about £45 and will last between six and nine months before needing to be replaced. The alternative catering-grade griddle grills are four times the size, use up much more electricity and cost around £300. Suitable for a busy breakfast café, but we found unnecessary for our sandwich bar.

Second, and most obviously, your contact grill can be used for toasting various types of sandwich, including sliced bread, paninis, wraps and bagels. You'll find that toasted sandwiches are exceedingly popular, and that many people will come in looking specifically for a toasted lunch option. For this task you should again opt for good-quality domestic grills. If cleaned regularly, and switched off between uses, then you'll find you'll achieve about ten months' use out of each that you buy. We've found this solution to work perfectly for us, as the grills are compact and can toast four panini at a time, and are very cost-effective.

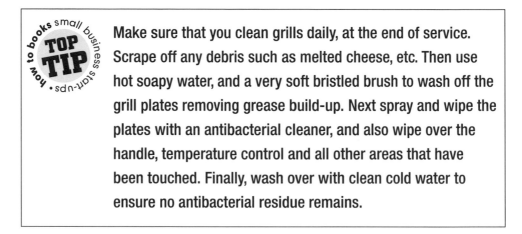

Make sure that you clean grills daily, at the end of service. Scrape off any debris such as melted cheese, etc. Then use hot soapy water, and a very soft bristled brush to wash off the grill plates removing grease build-up. Next spray and wipe the plates with an antibacterial cleaner, and also wipe over the handle, temperature control and all other areas that have been touched. Finally, wash over with clean cold water to ensure no antibacterial residue remains.

Hot water boiler

This is a free-standing unit which holds a reservoir of boiling water for making tea, and other hot drinks. Some units are plumbed into the water mains, while others, as in the case of the boiler we use, can be topped up with water each day manually from the tap.

Depending on your café and demands for hot drinks, you may or may not need a water boiler. We are able to serve all the hot drinks we need through the boiling water tap on our coffee machine, and never need use the reservoir within our water boiler. We keep it purely as back-up, in case our coffee machine breaks down, to enable us to at least continue to serve tea.

Soup kettle

If you're planning on serving soup through the winter months then I would wholeheartedly recommend you invest in one or two soup kettles. In lay terms, a soup kettle, or bain marie, is a huge heated flask that enables you to keep foodstuffs such as soup hot and ready to serve. They make lunch service so much easier, as when soup is ordered it can be served immediately, with no need to use a microwave for individual portions.

You should invest in a new soup kettle if your budget allows, as second-hand ones often have faulty elements and don't keep the contents of the kettle hot enough.

Prep benches

If you're making your own sandwich fillings, or pre-packing sandwiches, you'll need plenty of preparation space. There are some excellent value for money stainless steel preparation benches available from catering equipment suppliers such as Nisbets. This is the best option, as the benches will be hard-wearing and hygienic. Some are even collapsible, so you can use them during prep and then store them away, creating more space for lunchtime service.

Smoothie blender

As with all your equipment, you need to base your choice of blender on your business requirement. Are smoothies and milkshakes going to play a big part in your menu, or will they just be a sideline? Do you intend to serve more than ten per day, or will you be happy with one or two?

If you intend to make smoothies and shakes a profile item on your menu, then I would recommend investing in a commercial blender. We opted for Blendtec, as we noticed that all the big smoothie bar chains use this brand. The blender comes with a sound guard, which makes it much more café customer friendly! They are expensive; however, in two and half years of constant use we are yet to have a fault.

If on the other hand you know that smoothies will not play a big part in your menu, then you could consider a top of the range domestic smoothie blender instead. You'll find that they are a quarter of the price of the commercial blenders, and yet can withstand a fair bit of wear and tear.

Food processor

If you plan to make many of your sandwich fillings and accompaniments, rather than buying them in ready-made, then a good food processor will be vital. I would recommend you consider a commercial brand such as Magi-mix (used by Jamie Oliver, Gordon Ramsay *et al.*); commercial appliances can take the strain of constant use, and are big enough to cope with the quantities of food you'll be preparing.

Café Culture

We spent £600 on a food processor, which seemed like a massive amount of money at the time. However, it has delivered return on investment many times over, as during the past two and a half years it has powered its way through tonnes of carrots, cabbage, bacon, chicken and eggs to make many of our handmade salads and sandwich mixes. So far we've had to replace only one part, worth £35.

Oven

There are a number of uses for an oven in a sandwich bar, primarily cooking jacket potatoes, baking off bread and cooking food such as roasted vegetables for sandwich fillings. When fitting out your café you need to decide whether to have specially designed ovens for each purpose (a potato baking oven, a bread bake-off oven, and a regular oven), or whether to simply have one oven for all your tasks.

☐ **Jacket potatoes** – In my experience, if you intend to sell around 30 jacket potatoes per day, then you can quite easily work with a domestic double oven. Use the bottom, larger oven to cook the potatoes from scratch at a high temperature, and the smaller, upper oven to hold cooked jackets at a lower temperature, ready to serve.

If you intend your sale of jacket potatoes to be significantly higher than this number, or want to market the jackets visually to your customers, then your other option is a specifically designed potato-baking oven. Usually this features a glass hot hold display case on top, to show the cooked jackets to customers. These are significantly more expensive, and would require designated counter-top space.

Café Culture

We invested in a standard electric double oven before opening our shop, and have used it each day since to cook jacket potatoes, and to oven roast vegetables for our sandwich fillings. In the early days we even baked off trays of croissants and pastries for breakfast. It has, so far, coped well with the rigours of everyday café life, and for the £180 investment has delivered outstanding value for money. For us, it simply is not necessary to invest four times that in commercial ovens.

☐ **Bread bake-off** – I know many sandwich bar owners who sing the praises of bake-off ovens, and sell large quantities of baguettes and croissants that they've baked from frozen in 20 minutes. I understand the benefits too; as a sandwich bar owner you are able to bake to meet demand. Many of the frozen part-baked breads available are of excellent quality, and the smell in the shop is truly mouth-watering.

However, we tried bake-off in our first few months, selling croissants and Danish pastries cooked in our oven, to no avail. While it may work for some sandwich bars, customers in our locality simply were not interested, and produce went to waste. For this reason I would suggest that you trial bake-off with a small selection of breads, and using your basic oven, before investing in a specifically designed bake-off oven, and lots of frozen stock.

Fly killer

Necessary in any food-related business. These are wall-mountable units that give off a blue light, thus attracting all flying creatures buzzing about your shop. The tray collects their various little corpses, and you'll need to clean it out (probably the worst job you'll ever do!) every five months or so.

A fly killer should not be placed near, or over, food preparation areas, and not too close to a door or window as this renders it useless. Your electrician can advise on which size and model to invest in and will install it for you.

Heating/air conditioning unit

Keeping your sandwich bar at a pleasant temperature will be a constant struggle. On the one hand you have various fridges, freezers and coffee machines kicking out hot air and vapour. One the other hand you have the door open much of the time as customers' come and go.

If the shop you have chosen for your venture already has air conditioning fitted into the ceiling then fantastic – this will enable you to regulate the temperature relatively effectively, and heat and cool the shop as required. However, if you don't have the advantage of existing air conditioning, you'll be faced with a hefty initial investment to install it (we recently got a quote for our 1,000 sq ft shop of £8,000), and this may mean that it is not a viable option for your unit.

Other alternatives for cooling during the summer months include; portable air conditioning units (also very expensive at around £800 per month), tower fans (more effective and space-saving than traditional round fans), and water-cooled fans (blowing air across an internally held reservoir of iced water and thus blowing cooler air around the shop).

During the winter months it may be necessary to heat the shop, particularly if you have a large seating area for customers. You might consider a heat curtain, mounted above the shop door, or recessed into the ceiling. This blows out warm air, and when positioned over the door ensures that no more cold air enters the shop.

Café Culture

For a large part of the year we function perfectly without heating or air conditioning. However, for around two months of winter our shop becomes teeth-chatteringly cold, and for a similar length of time during summer it becomes unbearably hot.

We have installed a heat curtain above the door, and during the winter months, so long as we switch it on as soon as we arrive, it works perfectly at keeping the café comfortably warm.

During the summer we install a number of tower fans, set to blow around the service areas in the shop and keep the staff cooler. We've found that it's not so vital to keep customer areas cool, as customers are relaxing with a cold drink, usually in the draft of the open doors. Staff on the other hand are working flat out, opening hot ovens and toasting sandwiches.

The odd one or two people complain that it's either too hot or too cold, but unfortunately the British weather means that we'd see absolutely no return on an £8,000 investment in air conditioning, and so the current solution is the one we'll stick with.

Alarm Bell

When using fans to cool the shop, take care that the air stream is not blowing warm air into the open serve-over counters and grab-and-go fridges. This will raise the internal temperature, and food could spoil.

Extractor fan

It is a requirement by law that your café has adequate ventilation, enabling the removal of cooking smells and fumes. I would suggest that you discuss what is deemed as 'adequate ventilation' with your hygiene inspector, as it could vary greatly from one café to another.

In our case, a domestic hood with circulating extractor fan was deemed sufficient. However in other cases you may be asked to install an air vent, running from the kitchen to outside of the café.

Microwave

Your microwave will be used heavily through lunchtime, particularly if you are serving jacket potatoes, and are required to heat portions of beans, chilli, melted cheese, etc. Suppliers such as Nisbets sell reasonably priced low-end commercial microwaves that are perfectly suited to life in a sandwich bar, and if cleaned daily and maintained well should last you four or five years.

Till

This will depend quite a lot on who the operators of the till are. If you plan on having lots of different staff using the till, then an advanced unit which makes the operation very simple, like touch-screen technology might be the best option. This kind of till unit will eradicate any mistyping or forgetting of costs for certain items, as it's all pre-programmed, and the operator simply presses 'latte' or 'cheese sandwich', for example. However, as this kind of sophisticated till unit starts at around £2,500 you will need to be certain that the investment is appropriate for your business.

If you already anticipate that you'll be staffing the till yourself, then perhaps all you need is a glorified calculator that adds up, prints receipts, etc. These till units start much cheaper around the £200 mark, and can be picked up easily online, or even some larger cash and carry wholesalers sell them. We purchased a Casio till unit for £230. We still use it today, and it is in perfect working order.

Alongside the till purchasing decision you may also be considering whether to accept credit and debit cards. This will depend on your target audience. If you plan to serve primarily office workers, and you anticipate your average spend per head will be under £10, then there is a general acceptance that because of the small transactional value you won't need to offer this service. However, if your café will be serving a large percentage of customers eating in, and you expect them to spend more per head, then you may need to enable them to pay electronically.

If you decide to provide this means of payment then you will have to invest in the machinery to do so, pay a handling fee on every transaction, and ensure that staffs using the till are trained properly. If you have only a couple of electronic transactions per day you may never recoup this investment. Ask yourself whether it is really worth allowing your margins to be affected in order to offer this convenience to a handful of customers.

In our case we don't offer electronic payment, and three years down the line we still feel this is the right decision. Yes, there are a few customers who grumble. But they soon nip to the cashpoint a few metres down the road when they see how yummy our food is!

Dishwasher

A well-made domestic dishwasher is the only really viable option for a sandwich bar, as commercial machines are extremely expensive and very large. We buy second-hand machines, ensuring that they have a 'quick wash' cycle of around 30 minutes. This cycle can cope perfectly well with the coffee cup/sandwich plate load through lunchtime, and is fast enough to ensure that your stocks of crockery do not run out.

Ensure that you thoroughly rinse out the filter in your dishwasher at the end of each day. And once a week I suggest that you use a dishwasher cleaning product designed to rinse through your machine, and clear out the tubes and jets. This way your domestic dishwasher can keep up with the five, six, or even seven mayo-filled loads it'll need to do per day, and you'll get around 12 months of life out of it before the door begins to crack or it becomes clogged and stops washing.

Make sure you have the contact details of various maintenance companies to hand. If your coffee machine breaks down, or the fridges are struggling to keep their temperatures, you need to have someone reliable who is able to get there pretty quickly. When purchasing your equipment, make enquiries about who your suppliers use or recommend.

Perhaps make some initial enquiries before you open your café, so that you understand call out times, and prices. The last thing you want to be doing is flicking through the Yellow Pages when you've got a shop full of customers waiting to be served!

PRACTICAL AND EFFICIENT WORKING

As well as pleasing your customers, your sandwich bar's design also needs to please you. This means it has to be practical and enable efficient working.

Practicality over beauty!

Yes, it's important that your sandwich bar's fixtures, fittings and décor are visually pleasing, but this should not be to the detriment of its practicality. You'll be amazed at the amount of everyday wear and tear every item in your sandwich bar will have to deal with. Consider whether an item is easy to clean, is made of hard-wearing, chip-resistant material, is easily replaceable?

Efficient work flow

The key to any money-making sandwich bar is efficient working. You need to be able to serve as many customers as possible, in the most efficient way possible, during the golden hours of 12 noon to 2pm. To do this you need to map out work flow throughout your café. Is the equipment in the right place? Will a member of staff have to run half way across the kitchen to heat beans every time they serve a jacket potato? Will you have to dart into the kitchen to re-stock your coffee milk jugs, or will your milk supply be to hand? Think about it now and get it right from the start, because moving things around later will be a real headache.

We used reams of masking tape, and literally mapped out serve-over counters, prep stations and table and chairs on the floor of our empty shop unit before deciding on a final layout design. We walked around our imaginary café, discussing where bottle necks may occur, whether staff would have enough room to work, and where we could make improvements.

MANAGING THE RE-FIT

Once you've signed on the dotted line, and picked up the keys to your shop, the clock is ticking. For every day you're not trading, you are losing money. But with so much to do, how do you ensure that the re-fit is fast and professional, and that you open on the day you plan?

Establish exactly what works will be carried out

Changes to shop layout, building new partition walls, tiling the kitchen, fitting new electricity sockets, fitting new ceiling tiles, painting walls, installing a water boiler, fitting a new circuit board, laying new flooring, fitting kitchen units, installing a new WC, hanging lighting, installing a new shop fascia, installing new kitchen equipment. The amount of work you'll need to do will depend on the decorative state of your shop unit, and the final look you're hoping to achieve. The important thing is to decide, before you sign on the dotted line, exactly how much work needs to be carried out, and have a realistic understanding of the cost of this work.

Decide who'll do the work

In our experience it is more cost-effective to pay a builder, decorator, etc. to carry out the work, rather than attempting to save pennies by doing it yourself. It'll be far more beneficial to the business if you're focused on the opening – dealing with suppliers, hiring staff – rather than painting walls and tiling. With this in mind it's highly likely that you'll need to forge relationships with a builder, decorator, electrician and plumber. It's best to begin establishing these relationships sooner rather than later.

A streamlined approach is to appoint a builder as the main contractor, and then use the services of the electricians, plumbers and decorators who work with him or her. This saves you time, as you don't need to source each individual trade yourself.

☐ **Ask around**. Do any of your friends know of a reputable builder? Keep your eyes and ears open – are there any shops being re-fitted locally, or have any been re-fitted or decorated recently?

☐ **Get two or three quotes**. Once you have a shortlist of builders, meet with them individually on site at the shop, discuss your requirements, timelines and budgets. Ask them to provide you with a detailed quote, and to flag up areas where costs may change once the re-fit commences. Ideally the quote will be broken down into the various tasks, rather than one big lump sum. This way you can see how much each item of work costs, and decide how to prioritize your budget.

☐ **Make your decision**. This should be based on three factors: cost, professionalism and personality. It's important to keep costs to a minimum, but you also need to believe that the work carried out will be on time and to a high standard, and your relationship with the builder needs to be honest and open.

☐ **Create a schedule of work**. Once you've chosen your builder, hold a planning meeting, and schedule all the work to be carried out. Ensure that both you and your builder agree to this schedule of works, and that your deadline is agreed upon. Post a large copy of this schedule of works on the wall in your shop, highlighting important deadlines.

☐ **Final budget**. Once the schedule of work is set, and the other trades have had a chance to provide your builder with estimates for their areas of work, you will be able to agree on a final budget. Get budget guarantees for as many parts of the work as possible. This does not mean that the re-fit will be exactly on budget, but it does mean that you'll have a greater chance of winning a major dispute if one arises.

☐ **Project management**. You should visit your shop every day to ensure that work is progressing at the pace demanded by the schedule of works. Make sure that you are constantly receiving updates from your builder, and that he or she is keeping you informed of any delays, issues, problems or potential increases in budget. Perhaps organize a formal catch-up meeting at the end of each week, where these matters can be raised, and solutions discussed. This does not have to be formal, just a 20-minute chat over a cup of tea.

☐ **Be gutsy**. Imagine that the builder is supposed to have finished erecting a new partition wall in time for the electrician to hard wire it with new cables for electricity sockets. You arrive at the shop to find the wall is still only part-way built. The builder is at another job, and thought it'd be OK to finish the wall tomorrow. The electrician's task is now delayed by two days, which will have a knock-on effect on the decorator, who was scheduled to tile and paint the wall, and so on and so on. You have to be in control and assertive. If you've taken control from the outset, and have a firm schedule of works, it is far les likely that your tradespeople will mess you around. However, you can't ease up on the pressure for a moment, and need to keep noses to the grindstone until the job is finished.

☐ **Snagging**. Only sign off the job when you're absolutely certain that each and every item on your schedule of works has been completed to the standard you expect. Snagging is the term for the little finishing touches: paint chips here, wonky sockets there. Make sure you carry out a snagging inspection, and provide a final task list to your builder.

☐ **Keep talking**. If the final invoice comes in and there are costs included that weren't part of the original budget then talk to your builder about it. Ask for an explanation of the costs, and a breakdown of where the money was spent. It may be that you overlooked something, or it may be that the builder has accidentally charged you twice. Either way, the only way to sort things out is to discuss it.

Café Culture

We had an excellent builder and team of tradespeople; however, communication regarding deadlines still came unstuck. Two weeks prior to opening we were on site and chatting to our electrician. He happened to mention that he had four weeks remaining on the project, before he began his next. This would mean he finished our shop two weeks after we were due to open!

Thanks goodness we caught this mistake early! We put the building team right, and he worked late into the night for the next two weeks, in order to meet our deadline, and we opened on time thanks to his dedication!

Hire an architect. It may seem excessive and unnecessary to hire an architect, but in our experience having a clearly drawn out plan is key to a smooth re-fit process. How else will the builder know exactly where to put the wall, where the various electricity sockets are going to go, where the sink should be plumbed in, where lighting should be installed?

We approached a number of local independent architects who advertised on www.yell.com. The one we chose offered the basic services we needed, and could draw up our plans for a very reasonable budget (about £400).

Establishing your kitchen – hygiene and the law

Good food hygiene and food safety management is imperative if you want your business to be professional and successful. First, it helps you to obey the law; second, it reduces the risk of food poisoning among your customers; and third, it protects your business's reputation.

It's probably best if you accept very early on that this is a matter of the utmost importance, and that unlike your menu, your brand, or the colour of your walls, you have no 'creative licence' when it comes to how you should and should not work. That's why, before you receive your first delivery, mix your first batch of tuna mayonnaise, or serve your first customer, you should take the time to understand the regulations that apply to you, and to create and document a set of food safety management procedures to work to. Then you will be safe in the knowledge that your sandwich bar is operating within the law.

FIRST THINGS FIRST – UNDERSTANDING THE LAW

The law surrounding the production and sale of food can seem a bit of a minefield, and to the untrained eye it's often hard to understand what is and is not relevant. For you, opening a sandwich bar café, the most important food hygiene regulations that apply are:

☐ Regulation (EC) 852/2004 on the hygiene of foodstuffs.

☐ The Food Hygiene (England) Regulations 2006 (as amended) and equivalent regulations in Scotland, Wales and Northern Ireland.

☐ General Food Law Regulation (EC) 178/2002.

☐ General Food Regulations 2004.

Together, these regulations set out the basic hygiene requirements for all aspects of your sandwich bar business. This includes your premises and facilities, processes and practices, staff and training. The regulations also include temperature control requirements, the requirement to put in place 'food safety management' procedures, and guidelines for which daily records your are required to keep. In addition, they also state that you must make sure that the food your sandwich bar sells is safe, and that its consumption will not be harmful to people's health.

The good news is that you're not expected to read all these regulatory and legal documents in detail, nor should you worry about creating a multitude of 'all new' practices and processes to ensure that your sandwich bar is operating legally. In fact, I would advise that you do quite the opposite.

The most straightforward and foolproof way to ensure that your sandwich bar complies with the law is by following one of the Food Standards Agency (FSA) food safety management packs available to small catering businesses. In England and Wales this is the *Safer Food, Better Business* pack, in Scotland

CookSafe, and in Northern Ireland *Safe Catering*. You can order these packs via www.food.gov.uk or by contacting your local authority.

The FSA's *Starting Up – Your first steps to running a catering business*, and *Food Hygiene – A guide for businesses* are also both extremely useful. The latter provides a simple, easy to understand overview of the key laws that will affect your business, what they require you to do, and how they will be enforced.

THE BIG ISSUE – HANDLING FOOD SAFELY

I've listed some of the main hygiene and food management areas that will be relevant to you and your sandwich bar, so that you can start to understand the scale of your responsibility and the issues you'll need to consider.

Hazard Analysis Critical Control Point (HACCP)

Put simply, HACCP is a method of managing food safely. It all about putting in place procedures in order to control any hazards (harmful bacteria, chemical cleaning products, glass shards, etc. that the food you serve may come in contact with). Some people think HACCP is very complicated, but in truth it's not. It's just a set way of looking at what you do, considering any risks, and making sure that you put practices in place to avoid those risks.

The law says that you must put in place 'food safety management procedures' based on the principles of HACCP. In practice in your sandwich bar this means that you need to consider any hazards to the food you serve, and then put procedures in place to manage these hazards. You must also write down these procedures, keep them updated, and ensure they are available for the EHO to check on a visit to your premises.

Café Culture

A hazard could be anything from a staff member's hair falling into the food as they prepare it to sausages being cooked on a grill that is dirty. As part of our HACCP planning we recognized issues such as these, and through documentation of our staff hygiene code (requiring hair to be tied back) and our cleaning procedures (stipulating the method of thorough hygienic cleaning required after the grill's morning breakfast use) we comply with the law.

Personal hygiene

Personal hygiene is obviously very important, and you and your staff must follow simple rules to make sure that you do not contaminate the food in any way. This includes making sure hair is tied back, not wearing jewellery (expect a wedding band), and not touching the face, chewing gum, eating or sneezing when preparing food.

HACCP! All those weird letters may sound like gobbledegook! But don't worry, all you need to do is follow the worksheets within an approved FSA guide, such as *Safer Food, Better Business*, in order to ensure you comply with the law.

The law states that you and your staff should wear 'suitable' and where necessary protective clothing. What is deemed 'suitable' and when 'protective' clothing is required is dependent on each individual case; however, industry best practice dictates that your staff at least wear aprons and blue latex gloves when handling food.

You must not allow any of your staff to come to work if they are suffering from or carrying a disease that is likely to be transmitted through food, if they have infectious skin wounds or sores, and if they have sickness and diarrhoea.

Alarm Bell

Staff with sickness and/or diarrhoea should not return to work until they have had no symptoms for 48 hours.

The four Cs

Good food hygiene is all about the four Cs: **cross-contamination**, **cleaning**, **chilling and cooking**. By controlling the four Cs you control harmful bacteria, and thus control the thing that causes serious illness.

☐ **Cross-contamination** – This is when bacteria are spread between food, surfaces or equipment. A likely cause is when raw food touches (or perhaps drips into) ready-to-eat food, equipment or surfaces. It is one of the common causes of food poisoning.

It is possible to prevent it through consistent and thorough cleaning of work stations and hands, by using different preparation boards and knives for different food types, and by keeping raw and ready-to-eat foods apart at all times.

☐ **Cleaning** – Effective cleaning gets rid of bacteria on hands, equipment and surfaces. This in turn helps prevent bacteria spreading onto food. Make sure that your staff always wash and dry their hands thoroughly before handling food. They should also clean food preparation areas in between tasks, especially after handling raw foods, and clean and clear as they go, making sure equipment and surfaces are sanitized before the next task is begun.

This sounds like a big task, but it's not. Simply ensure that you have anti-bacterial spray cleaner and a paper towel dispenser located in your kitchen, and the task of hygienically cleaning the prep areas after each task becomes so much easier!

☐ **Chilling** – Chilling food properly helps to stop harmful bacteria from growing, and some foods need to be chilled in order to keep them safe. It's really important that you don't leave chilled foods standing around at room temperature, as this could mean it becomes unsafe to eat.

Make sure you check the temperature of chilled food on delivery to make sure it is cold enough, and once you've checked it put it away in your fridge straight away. You should also keep a close eye on your fridge temperatures, and keep a log so that you can prove that they are within the safe temperature 'zone'.

☐ **Cooking** – Thorough cooking kills harmful bacteria. That's why it is really important that you ensure any foods you heat (baked beans, chilli for jacket potatoes) is piping hot, all the way through, before you serve it to a customer. Stir during heating, and check with a temperature probe.

Café Culture

If you're using a soup kettle or bain marie, check the temperature of the food it holds regularly during service. All it takes is for the lid to be left open a little too long, or the temperature knob to be accidentally adjusted, and you'll be serving food that is not hot enough.

We heat our soups on the hob, ensuring they are 160 degrees all the way through, before decanting them into the soup kettles just before lunch begins at 11.45am. This way, the kettles can keep the soup boiling hot and ready for each portion to be served swiftly and safely. Although the instructions that came with the kettle stated that cold soup can be placed inside the kettle and left to heat slowly during the morning, we did not find this to be the case. The soups never became thoroughly piping hot, and we'd rather not risk it!

Establishing your kitchen – food preparation and stock control

I know of café owners who 'fly by the seat of their pants', who leave it until the last minute to decide how much stock to order, or food to produce. Needless to say, their businesses are not as successful as they could be, and they're always complaining about how stressful their life is.

It does not need to be this way. Just because you own the business, it does not mean you have to be stressed, frantic, frazzled, or any other of those horrible words. After all, you're hoping to achieve a better work-life balance, right?

By working in an organized, structured and methodical way you can be in control of your kitchen and therefore your business, and not let it be in control of you. Here are some key areas where you can take control.

FOOD PREPARATION

How do you know how much tuna mayo to prepare or order in for any given day's trading? How many tomatoes should you slice, how much lettuce should you wash? It's tough when you first open, and of course you will sometimes get it wrong.

The good news is that you're not completely in the dark, and you do have information at your fingertips that can help you guesstimate how much food you'll need to prepare. Your business plan should tell you roughly how many customers you anticipate serving in your opening weeks, and in addition you'll also know which sandwiches on your menu will appeal to the masses, and which will be more specialist. Finally, you'll know how many sandwiches you'll be able to make from one batch of any given sandwich filling.

This information should give you the ability to create an informed schedule for food preparation and food ordering for your first few weeks of trading. After that, you'll be in a position to base production and ordering on customers' buying trends, and you'll develop a 'feel' for how much of each product will sell on any given day.

STOCK ORDERING

You can use the same 'guesstimate' method for stock ordering as is outlined above for food preparation. However, be careful in the first few weeks not to over-order produce that has a short shelf life, such as bottles of fresh apple juice. It can be a costly exercise to have to throw away half a crate when they remain unsold beyond the use-by date on their lids. Just ensure that your stocks of longer-life produce, such as cans of drinks, bottles of water, crisps and chocolate are always plentiful.

> **TOP TIP**
> *how to books small business start-ups*
>
> I would recommend that you create a 'prep list', documenting all the sandwich fillings, jacket fillings and salad items that you serve. At the end of a day's service check through each of the fridges and serve-over counters and make a note of what you have left, and is in date for sale the following day. Then, from this stock level, decide what needs to be prepared the following morning, and log this amount on the prep list. When you or your staff come into work the next day there'll be a structured approach to the preparation, and you'll be certain that the correct amount is being made.

As mentioned earlier, a good way to ensure that stock ordering is organized is to document all suppliers and deliveries.

☐ First, create a list of all the suppliers you'll be using, their order days, delivery days and contact telephone numbers. Mount this list somewhere prominent so that all staff can see it.

☐ Next, create a template order sheet for each supplier, listing all the products that you source from them.

☐ Now, every time you place an order, fill in an order sheet. You'll be able to keep track each day of what produce is on order, and when it is expected in.

☐ When it arrives you can check it off against your list, and be certain that everything you ordered has arrived.

☐ You can also train staff to begin an order sheet when they notice stock is running low, as there's nothing worse than running out of stock because no one realized it needed ordering.

LABELLING

The most efficient way to keep track of what food is in your fridges, and when its use-by date is up, is to label everything.

There is an array of food production labels available via catering suppliers and packaging companies. Some are colour-coded day stickers, enabling you to see at a glance which food goes out of date on the day in question. Others are larger labels, enabling more information to be documented, such as the initials of the member of staff who prepared the item, the date it was made, the quantity of the batch, and its use-by date. Either type is suitable for a sandwich bar, and will ensure that you are following food hygiene best practice, and keeping your environmental health officer happy!

Café Culture

Absolutely everything in our fridges has a label. This makes the task of managing stock, and food production so much simpler. At a glance my husband, myself or a member of staff can see how much we have left of a particular item of food, which batch should be used first, and when a batch goes out of date. If a batch is substandard we can see which member of staff prepared it, and re-train them accordingly. We love labels!

SUPERVISION AND TRAINING

As the owner of a sandwich bar you are legally required to ensure that all the food handling staff working for you are supervised and/or trained in food hygiene matters related to their job. This does not mean that you need to send each and every member of staff on an external food hygiene and management course, but it does mean that you should undertake a suitable course yourself, and that you should then instruct your staff in all the essential areas of food hygiene and management that is relevant to them.

This might be a legal requirement, but even if it were not, I would still recommend you do the same anyway. Why? Because trained staff follow the processes you've put in place to keep your kitchen organized and efficient. Untrained staff do not, and that causes business chaos and puts you under stress.

I recommend that you include the hygiene and food management matters that you feel are relevant to your staff within your staff handbook. You could also perhaps develop a 'new starter' training handout, to ensure you cover the important hygiene training with each and every new member of staff.

Health and safety

Health and safety has become a bit of an 'in' joke, and there certainly seem to be a multitude of new rules and regulations that often seem a tad unnecessary for the independent sandwich bar. However, rules are rules . . . and often you simply need to be able to prove that you've undertaken a short assessment, and that you're aware of the risks, in order to comply.

FIRE PROTECTION

You'll need to undertake an assessment of the specific risk that fire poses in your sandwich bar, and be able to show that you have controls in place. The fire safety officer at your local fire station can provide you with the details, and will visit your premises and undertake an informal inspection. Your shop will need to have a set escape route for customers and staff, fire-resistant doors and walls, firefighting equipment (extinguishers), fire alarms, emergency lighting, safe storage of flammable materials and staff training.

It is the responsibility of employers to ensure that their staff are adequately trained on what to do in the event of fire. Training should be given upon induction and preferably a second time within the first month of employment. In the case of your sandwich bar this could mean that you simply show a member of staff where the fire escape is (perhaps the only door in and out of your business), and what to do in the event of a fire (alert you, or the manager).

DISABLED ACCESS

You'll need to make 'reasonable' adjustments to your sandwich bar if disabled people would otherwise find it impossible or difficult to access it. This could mean making sure a table is not blocking the entrance so that a wheelchair user could come in unaided, or changing your 'no animals' policy, to enable a customer with a guide dog to sit and eat. The most important thing is that you review your sandwich bar with disabled people in mind. Create a short document on the computer, simply listing the issues that may arise, and outline where possible how you might make adjustments, or where adjustment would be too difficult or costly.

MANAGING WASTE

Your business is responsible for any waste it creates. You must ensure that you are able to store it in suitable sacks, bins or containers, and that it is collected from your business by an authorized contractor, such as the local council waste collectors.

Café Culture

Fire safety does not have to be a mammoth task. Our local fire safety officer was incredibly helpful, and advised us on how many fire alarms were necessary, and where to install them. In addition, we employed a local fire safety firm to fit our fire extinguishers and blankets, and provide training. Now they come back once a year to conduct the annual safety tests – nice and easy, no big deal!

RISK ASSESSMENT

The Health and Safety at Work Act sets out general guidelines for health and safety and requires every business, no matter how small, to conduct a risk assessment. You should consider the risks posed to your customers when visiting your shop, and to your staff when working a shift. This should include a range of hazards such as slips, trips and falls, manual handling of loads, using hot equipment, using sharp knives. The important thing for you to decide is whether a hazard is significant, and whether you have it covered by satisfactory precautions. This risk assessment needs to be written down if you employ more than four people.

The Health and Safety Executive's website is really easy to follow. Visit www.hse.gov.uk and print off lots of helpful guides on all the areas mentioned in this section.

INSURANCE

As a sandwich bar owner you must insure against claims arising from any harm caused to your staff while they are working for you. **Employers' liability insurance**, which protects your business against claims from employees for accidents, injuries or sickness they may suffer as a result of working for you, is a legal requirement. The statutory minimum cover is £5 million, and you should display the certificate in your sandwich bar. I suggest you keep certificates even after they have expired, as employees could make a claim many years after they worked for you.

Sandwich bar businesses are not obliged to insure against the effects of any harm they may cause to the public, but some choose to do so. **Public liability insurance** covers claims made following an incident related to your business's property, premises or staff. Product liability insurance protects against claims following incidents caused by the food you've sold. **Professional indemnity insurance** covers your business against legal action taken by a customer.

It's best to talk to your insurance broker or financial adviser before deciding on the usefulness of these insurances to your sandwich bar.

INFORMING STAFF

If you have staff, even one or two, then you must have a health and safety policy and keep employees up to date and involved in your health and safety procedures. This could mean listing all the hazards a member of staff might come in contact with while at work, and outlining things they must not do, for fear of injury. Perhaps pin this up on the staff noticeboard, or include in a handbook. You must also have procedures in place in case of fire or other emergencies. You should display the poster 'Health and Safety Law: What You Should Know' in your sandwich bar for all staff to see.

REPORTING INCIDENTS

The Reporting of Injuries, Diseases and Dangerous Occurrences Regulations (RIDDOR) require you to keep records of accidents and other workplace incidents. The simplest way to meet this requirement is to have an accident book that sits on a shelf in your sandwich bar. All accidents and near misses should be jotted down, making sure you include the date and time of the incident, a true account of what happened, and who was involved, plus their signature. Make sure this information is kept for three years (a legal requirement).

FIRST AID TRAINING

Every organization in the UK has responsibilities according to the Health and Safety (First Aid) Regulations 1981. However, the scale of training you are required to have very much depends on the size of your business and the work you carry out.

The vast majority of sandwich bars and cafés would fall into the low-risk group. This means that the first aid provision that you'd be required to make is for one member of staff to be trained in first aid. There are a variety of courses available; one of the most established training providers is the British Red Cross. They run one-day courses, suitable for new sandwich bar owners, around the country. The cost for such a course is about £120, and you would be provided with a certificate valid for three years. Visit www.redcrossfirstaidtraining.co.uk.

4
OPENING AND THE EARLY DAYS

Understanding employment law

Because you're only intending to open a small sandwich bar, that will require one or two members of staff in the early days, employment law won't apply to you, right? Wrong!

I must admit we thought no differently. When we started our sandwich bar we were, like you, working flat out seven days a week to meet our opening date. We didn't realize just how many legal requirements came with employing staff, and didn't give enough time to employment law. The unfortunate truth is that we made a lot of mistakes in the early days.

We've learnt the hard way, and because of that we have taken the time to ensure that we get it right from now on. So, what are the main areas of employment law you should be aware of?

MINIMUM WAGE

It is a legal requirement that you pay your staff no less than the minimum wage. The rates at the time of writing (as of 1 October 2008) are:

☐ Youth rate (18–21 years): £4.77 per hour.

☐ Adult rate (22 years and over): £5.73 per hour.

The minimum wage regularly increases (usually in October), and you should visit the HM Revenue & Customs website (www.hmrc.gov.uk) to learn what the existing rate is, and whether there are plans for it to increase in the near future.

REST BREAKS

A worker is entitled to an uninterrupted break of 20 minutes when their daily working time is more than six hours. It should be a break in working time and should not be taken either at the start or at the end of a working day. If a young worker (aged 18–21) is required to work more than four and a half hours at a time, then they are entitled to a break of 30 minutes.

There is free guidance produced by the BERR (Department for Business, Enterprise and Regulatory Reform) or the DTI as was, which can provide more information. Visit www.berr.gov.uk and search on 'working time regulation'.

PAID HOLIDAY

All your staff are entitled to paid holiday. The main things to be aware of are:

Café Culture

We try to structure our shift patterns so that shifts are no longer than six hours. This means that legally we are not required to give staff a break. This may sound harsh, but as a small business it is difficult to find the budget to pay not only the minimum wage but also holiday and sick leave, plus have enough to pay yourself. You need to watch the pennies and keep staff wage expenditure on a tight rein. Paying staff to take breaks is something you should avoid, if you can.

☐ Your staff are currently entitled to a minimum of 4.8 weeks' paid holiday (from 1 October 2007), although this entitlement increases to 5.6 weeks from 1 April 2009.

☐ Those working part-time are entitled to the same level of holiday pro rata, i.e. 4.8 (5.6 from April 2009) times their usual working week.

☐ Your staff start building up holiday as soon as they begin work.

☐ As an employer you can control when your staff take their holiday. So, if you intend on closing for a week over Christmas, you can specify in their contracts that they save six days for this holiday period. You can also refuse a holiday leave request if another member of staff already has time booked off, or your business workload prevents it.

☐ When a member of staff leaves, you must calculate what holiday they have accrued pro rata, and ensure this payment is included within their final wage packet.

☐ You can include bank and public holidays within your employee's holiday entitlement.

If, like us and the vast majority of sandwich bars, you intend to employ part-time staff, or staff who work shifts, then you had better prepare yourself for a bit of mathematical science when working out how much paid holiday they are entitled to. We follow a system designed to calculate a 'holiday rate' for each individual member of staff. This is the system we use:

☐ **Step 1** – Decide what your 'working week' constitutes. This is the number of days your café is open. In our case it is a six-day week, Monday–Saturday.

☐ **Step 2** – Set a date as the beginning of your business's holiday year. This could be 1 April, for example.

☐ **Step 3** – Look back over the past 12 weeks of an employee's shift pattern. Calculate the average number of days they have worked per week. For this example we'll say that the member of staff in question has worked, on average, three days per week. Note, that weeks when the staff member was on holiday or off sick should not be used as 'example' weeks. The 12 weeks should be 12 'true' weeks.

☐ **Step 4** – Multiply their average week by 4.8 (5.6 from April 2009). In this case, 3 multiplied by 4.8, equals 14.5. So 14.5 is the number of paid days' holiday the member of staff in question is entitled to.

☐ **Step 5** – Next you need to calculate how much this member of staff will be paid for each of their 14.5 days' holiday. Look back again over the past 12 weeks. Calculate the average number of hours the member of staff has worked per shift. Let's say this figure is six. This means that for each day's holiday the member of staff will be paid for six hours, at their usual contracted hourly rate of pay.

☐ **Step 6** – Ensure that holiday pay is included in the pay packet following their leave, and keep track of how many days each member of staff is owed and has taken.

☐ **Step 7** – Pay staff any owing holiday when they resign. For example, if the member of staff has worked for you for six months, then they are entitled to seven days' paid holiday. If during their employment they have taken three days' holiday, then you must ensure that the remaining four days' pay are included within their final wages.

I recommend that you set a date each year to calculate your employees' annual holiday entitlement, and then give them the details so that they can plan annual holidays etc. Perhaps this date could be a week or so before the beginning of the new holiday year. Produce a 'holiday' statement for each member of staff, telling them how many days they'll be entitled to, and how much they'll be paid for each day they take off.

You won't be able to do this straight away, as employees won't have a 12-week shift schedule to look back through. As soon as you can, however, you should.

CONTRACTS AND WRITTEN PARTICULARS

As an employer you must provide your employees with a written contract within their first two months. Alongside this contract you must provide written statements of the grievance, disciplinary and dismissal procedures we as employers must follow. There are a number of ways you can develop this contract and the legal statements.

First, you could create them yourself. We found that Business Link's website (www.businesslink.gov.uk) is particularly easy to understand, plus it outlines the important areas for employers to get right. The ACAS website (www.acas.org.uk) is also very helpful.

The basic points a contract should cover are as follows:

- ☐ The names of the employee and employer.

- ☐ The place of work.

- ☐ The date when employment began.

- ☐ The rate of pay, and when and how wages will be paid.

- ☐ Hours of work (possibly flexible and part-time).

- ☐ Entitlement to sick leave, including any entitlement to sick pay.

- ☐ The entitlement of employer and employee to notice of termination.

- ☐ Job title and a brief description of the responsibilities of the role.

- ☐ When employment is not permanent, the period for which the employment is expected to last.

- ☐ Details of your disciplinary and grievance procedures.

- ☐ Information of any pensions or pension schemes.

Second, you could use an example contract, as provided by your local job centre (you can be sure that it meets all the legal requirements). Or alternatively use the expertise of a firm such as Croner Consulting (www.croner.co.uk), who are able to develop a contract, specifically for your business, for a fee of around £150. You'll then also receive their monthly newsletter, keeping you up to date with any employment law changes, such as increases to the amount of holiday your staff are entitled to, minimum wage increases and new legislation that could affect you. We find this particularly useful.

Café Culture

When we first opened and employed our first staff, we used contracts that we'd developed quickly ourselves. The contracts were based on various templates we'd sourced, and included sections on wages, holiday pay and termination of employment. To the untrained eye they looked as a contract should.

However, a few months after opening I decided to dedicate some serious time to getting to grips with employment law. I soon became aware that our contracts were lacking in many areas, and that because of this we were leaving ourselves wide open to the risk of a tribunal claim. I wasted no time in hiring a professional to re-work them, to make sure that every legal requirement was met, and that as a business we were without reproach.

The cost was worth it. Now, I use the same professional to re-work the contracts each year, taking into account any changes to the law. As a business we are protected, and our staff know that we take their employment seriously.

Alarm Bell

An employment tribunal case is something you want to avoid at all costs. Make sure that your employment practices are legal and that there are no loopholes that unscrupulous members of staff could capitalize on.

It costs them nothing to bring a claim against you. You on the other hand will be saddled with solicitor's fees (anywhere from £1,500 upwards), barrister costs (£1,500 upwards) and a final settlement figure if the employee is found to have a case against you (£2,000 and upwards).

MATERNITY LEAVE

The likelihood is that many of your staff will be female; this is just the nature of the industry. Because of this you need to be aware of and prepared for the responsibilities of providing maternity leave to your female employees.

All pregnant employees and new mothers – regardless of length of service or the hours they work – are entitled to paid time off for ante-natal care, normal sick pay rights for pregnancy-related sickness, and 52 weeks' maternity leave. For financial reasons many women choose not to take the full 52 weeks; however, you should assume that they would, unless they advise you otherwise.

Your staff member is required to inform you of their pregnancy 15 weeks before the beginning of the week their baby is due. Ask them for this notice in writing, and ensure that they provide you with the baby's due date, the date they wish to begin their maternity leave (can be up to 11 weeks before due date) and a copy of form MAT B1, supplied by their doctor or midwife, for your records. You then have 28 days in which to respond to their notice. Your letter should acknowledge when their maternity leave will start, and confirm the date of its end.

Members of staff on maternity leave can change their minds part-way through and decide to return earlier, or later, than originally planned. Again, ask for any such change request in writing.

Your sandwich bar workload will most certainly demand that you replace the member of staff on maternity leave with an additional member of staff. In this instance you should employ someone on a 'fixed term contract', making him or her aware that they are covering maternity leave. As the length of maternity leave can change part-way through it is advisable to set the fixed term contract on a rolling basis, perhaps in four-monthly blocks. Make sure you have outlined the terms of their contract in writing.

Once the member of staff returns from maternity leave they have the right to request flexible working. You are legally obliged to consider their request fairly, taking into consideration whether their hours can be reduced, and whether job-sharing is a possibility.

You should visit www.acas.org.uk and www.direct.gov.uk to find out what current maternity leave legislation requires of you.

STATUTORY MATERNITY PAY

Alongside your obligation to provide maternity leave to female employees, you'll also be required to provide Statutory maternity pay (SMP). This is designed to replace your employee's normal earnings to help her take time off around the time of the birth.

Whether you have to pay SMP to an expectant employee depends on how long they've worked for you and how much they earn. They'll have to provide you with evidence of when the baby is due and give you notice of when they want you to start paying their SMP. Remember that payments of SMP count as earnings. You must deduct tax and national insurance contributions (NICs) from them in the usual way.

For most sandwich bars this financial obligation is of real concern, as you'll also need to find the money to pay the new member of staff replacing the one on maternity leave. However, you can often recover some or all of the SMP you pay. Visit www.hmrc.gov.uk to find out more, and view the statutory maternity pay (SMP) section. You can also call the Inland Revenue employers' helpline on 08457 143 143.

PATERNITY/PARTNER'S LEAVE

Fathers/partners are also eligible for leave around the birth of a baby. They can take up to two weeks' leave, any time up to 56 weeks after the birth of the baby. Their statutory pay for the time off is either £117.18 or 90 per cent of average weekly earnings, whichever is the least amount. To be eligible they need to have worked 26 weeks' continuous service ending with the fifteenth week before the week the baby is due, and they must earn at least £90 per week. They should provide notice to you in writing before the end of the fifteenth week before the baby is due.

There is also legislation governing the rights of adoptive parents to take leave and receive statutory pay. Visit www.acas.org.uk and www.businesslink.gov.uk to find out more.

STATUTORY SICK PAY

If a member of your staff is off sick for four days or more then they will be eligible for statutory sick pay (SSP). You are not required to pay SSP for the first three days they take off. The payment of SSP continues for a maximum of 28 weeks, after which the employee can claim incapacity benefit from the DSS. The current weekly rate of SSP for days of sickness (from 6 April 2008) is £75.40.

As an employer you're responsible for operating the SSP scheme. You'll need to:

☐ Work out whether an employee meets the qualifying conditions (more below).

☐ Calculate how much SSP they're due.

☐ Pay the SSP to them.

☐ Keep a record of the SSP you pay.

If you keep paying your employees their normal wage when they're sick – and you pay them at least as much as the SSP they'd get – you don't have to operate the SSP scheme. However, you must put your sickness policy in a written statement of employment particulars and give a copy to all employees who have worked for you for at least a month.

Café Culture

We have our sickness policy in our staff handbook. It outlines that staff are eligible to statutory sick pay. It also outlines how staff must notify us when they are sick, and by when (i.e. via a telephone conversation with myself or my husband, and no later than one and a half hours before the start of a shift). It explains that within seven days of the first sickness the employee should complete a self-certification form regarding their situation, and in addition they must provide a medical certificate.

The self-certification form, SC2, is downloadable from the internet. It's useful if you have a number printed off for staff to fill in. Visit www.hmrc.gov.uk/forms/sc2.

Thankfully for you, as a small business owner, most of the money paid out can be claimed back from the government. This depends however, on the amount of national insurance you pay. I suggest that you contact the Inland Revenue employers' helpline (08457 143 143) and discuss the current rates you're able to reclaim.

The HM Revenue & Customs guide *Calculating and Recovering Statutory Sick Pay* is also worth reading, as is their help book E14, *What to do if your employee is sick*.

STAKEHOLDER PENSIONS

Not all sandwich bars will be required to offer a stakeholder pension scheme. If you employ five or more people, however, then you will.

It sounds like a really complicated and expensive business. But don't worry, it's not. A stakeholder pension is just a type of low-charge pension. You can buy a stakeholder pension from a commercial financial services company, such as a bank, insurance company or building society. Your obligation is simply to provide your employees with access to the scheme. It's up to them whether or not they contribute, and you don't need to contribute anything for them.

Café Culture

Our bank offers stakeholder pensions, so we decided to take one out through them. They provided us will all the information on the scheme, and helped us to draft a letter informing our staff of their option to begin contributing. At present none of our staff contribute, but that doesn't matter – we have met our legal obligations and offered them the opportunity.

GRIEVANCE PROCEDURES, DISCIPLINARY ACTION AND DISMISSAL

Unfortunately, even in the most well-run businesses there is sometimes cause for you to have a grievance with a member of staff, or they with you, or in extreme circumstances you may even need to discipline or dismiss someone. What's vital is that as an employer you follow the statutory grievance, discipline and dismissal procedures set out by law, because if you don't your member of staff will have the right to make an employment tribunal claim against you.

Grievances

If one of your employees has concerns or complaints about their work, employment terms, working conditions or relationships with colleagues, they may want to discuss them or bring them to your attention. They will then want you to address and, if possible resolve these grievances.

You are required by law to provide your staff with a written grievance procedure complying – at the very least – with the statutory grievance procedures (SGPs). The SGP is, roughly, as follows:

☐ Your employee must set out their grievance in writing.

☐ A meeting should be held (called a grievance hearing) so that you can talk to your staff member about their grievance and let them know the outcome. You need to organize this meeting as quickly as you can after you receive their letter. Once you've told them the outcome you also need to notify them of their right to appeal. The employee must appeal to complete the statutory procedure.

☐ If the member of staff is not happy with the outcome of the grievance hearing, they'll request an appeal meeting. After the meeting you should inform the employee of the decision taken, preferably in writing.

☐ The employee has the right to be accompanied to both meetings by a colleague or union representative. You should ensure that you make the staff member aware of this right.

116

Your grievance procedure will govern how you deal with a difficult member of staff, situation or staff complaint. It must be set out in writing, and it must comply with statutory grievance procedures.

Disciplinary rules

Your staff are the face of your business, and so it's really important to set clear rules of conduct, and have processes in place to act quickly if a member of staff is letting your business down. Again, as with grievance issues, you must make sure your rules are fair and clearly written and they must also reflect the needs of your business.

The positive thing about having rules is that they can help your workforce to understand what you expect of them, contain and resolve issues and help to avoid potential employment tribunal complaints. Your rules could cover a range of issues, including absence, health and safety, personal appearance, prohibited activities, smoking, alcohol and drugs, work standards and timekeeping.

The rules should also set out any behaviour that will be treated as gross misconduct – misconduct judged so serious that it's likely to lead to dismissal without notice. It's important to give examples of what will count as gross misconduct, such as: drunkenness/drug abuse, fighting at work, fraud, theft, gross negligence/insubordination, serious breaches of health and safety, and wilful damage to business property.

Disciplinary action

If you find that a member of staff has broken one of the rules, or is continually letting you down, then you may feel the need to take disciplinary action.

Your first step is to have an informal discussion with them, as soon as the problem arises. You should explain the problem and agree actions with them. This kind of informal chat is not part of any formal disciplinary procedure.

However, if your staff member's poor conduct or poor performance persists, you may have to take formal disciplinary action.

Just as with grievances, there is a standard approach you should follow. These are called statutory dismissal and disciplinary procedures (SDDPs). These procedures range from informal warnings, through to dismissal hearings, and should be followed to the letter.

Dismissal

At some stage you may face the undesirable task of having to dismiss an employee or a group of employees. As dismissal is such a serious outcome, you need to be sure that it's handled correctly; this will ensure that you avoid unfair, wrongful and constructive dismissal claims against you. Of course, effective recruitment, training and management from the start of employment will help you minimize the risk of poor performance, and therefore dismissal, but regardless, you do need to be prepared.

Again, there are statutory procedures in force that apply to many dismissals. As an employer you'll need to ensure that you follow these statutory dismissal procedures, and that the dismissal you carry out is fair and that you've acted reasonably. The following websites are worth exploring.

☐ www.businesslink.gov.uk has an excellent employment section, covering all aspects of employment law. It includes helpful guides to grievance, disciplinary and dismissal procedures, and what you should consider as an employer.

☐ www.acas.org.uk is also extremely useful. Its 'Tools' section includes example letters employers can use in correspondence with staff, and many helpful guidance documents. The ACAS helpline is also invaluable: 08457 47 47 47.

Café Culture

Before taking any HR related action I always call the ACAS helpline. I explain what I am intending to do, and ask whether or not they consider it to be the correct way to handle the situation. They are always very helpful and knowledgeable, and will make recommendations and provide advice.

Think of them as being your own free HR adviser.

Alarm Bell

Make sure you inform your business insurer before you begin any dismissal proceedings, as often legal fees relating to the case will be covered by your policy.

Hiring staff

First, let me just say that there are good employees out there! I feel I have to begin with this statement because during the recruitment process you are bound to become disheartened, as for every 20 CVs you receive, 18 will be useless. It's true that you might hit a 'vein' of excellent candidates, but usually there'll be a fair bit of dross along the way.

Remember, you'll train these people, you'll trust them, and you'll allow them to serve your precious customers. They need to be right.

FINDING CANDIDATES

So, how do you find these candidates? Well, there are conventional ways of advertising for staff: the local paper, job agencies and the local job centre. Truthfully, though, we've found the old-fashioned way of placing a poster in the café window works best. It'll take up less of your time, you'll get better-quality candidates, and it'll cost far less money. Plus, while your premises are being fitted out there'll be plenty of interest in what new shop is about to open! Make the most of this interest by utilizing your empty window space for posters.

Café Culture

As soon as we were handed the keys to our café we began advertising for staff. We used our designer to create a job advertisement poster. We made sure it was eye-catching and in keeping with our brand. It explained briefly what our café was all about, and gave details of anticipated hours of work. It asked interested candidates to email their CV, put a copy of their CV through the door, telephone, or to pop in and pick up an application form (if we were there).

In all, 85 people applied for the jobs, ranging from school-leavers to OAPs. Sometimes decent candidates are hard to find, other times you feel like there's an abundance! We recruited our first three members of staff from the in-café advertising.

Café Culture

Foreign staff contribute massively to the sandwich bar sector. In fact, one supplier of mine recently joked that if all the Polish people in London decided to go back home, then virtually every café would have to close! I'm not sure if that's really the case; however, I can be certain that you'll receive many applications from foreign workers.

Don't fear the prospect of having a mixed nationality workforce. In our experience foreign workers are committed and have an outstanding work ethic (particularly Polish workers, who we literally could not do without). Do ensure that recruits have a suitable level of spoken English, and make sure that you test it during the interview stage. There's nothing worse for the customer than having to repeat their order twice!

The key next is to be prepared. Not all people interested in general café assistant positions will have a pre-prepared CV. With this in mind you need to develop a set list of questions to ask interested candidates when they telephone you about the position. This will enable you to filter all the applications, and help you to decide who to invite for an interview. Ask for the following information:

☐ Person's full name, contact details and age.

☐ Where they are currently working, or where their last job was.

☐ The reason they left their last position.

☐ Why they want to work in a sandwich bar.

☐ What hours they are hoping to work.

☐ What experience they have that may be relevant.

If you consider the person to be a suitable candidate, invite them to an interview. Ideally this should take place at your sandwich bar, but if re-fit works prevent this, a nearby (competitor) coffee shop will do.

Café Culture

Of the 85 applications we received we considered eight to have potential – this is an average percentage. We conducted the interviews in a nearby Costa coffee shop, as our premises were a building site (literally!).

Alarm Bell

The interview process should be your filter. Don't let anyone through this process unless you're 80% happy with him or her, not even when you're desperate, and two weeks from opening!

I say 80%, not 100%, because in our experience you can never truly understand a candidate's personality and ability during the recruitment process, no matter how thorough. It takes a couple of really busy shifts in the café to reach that point!

Don't ignore any niggling doubts you have about people you interview at this stage. Even if they talk the talk, and look the part, if gut instinct is telling you they won't be right for your café then don't ignore it. You can't afford the time or the energy training someone who'll only last a month or so.

Once you're up and running, and employing new staff, you should consider asking interview candidates to work for a trial shift before you employ them – usually a couple of hours over the busiest time of the day, spent shadowing experienced members of staff. If they are successful, wages for the shift can be included in their first pay packet; otherwise their time should be voluntary.

Finally, don't expect the staff you employ for opening necessarily to be with you six months in. If they are, great! If, however, you find you made the wrong choice, and hired the wrong person, never mind. You're learning, and it's hard to find the right staff. You will become skilled at spotting a good worker from a bad one, and eventually be able to tell within minutes whether a candidate is right for the job.

EMPLOYEE INDUCTION

Once you've found the right person it's really important to welcome them professionally into your business. This not only helps them understand what is expected of them, but also protects you and your business and ensures that your HR practices are within the law.

We have found that the best way to stay on the right side of the law is to create a set of documents, used for all new members of staff, and to follow the same process each time someone is recruited. All the documents are saved as templates on the computer, and each time we recruit someone new we simply amend the template and save it into the new member of staff's own folder. That way nothing gets missed or forgotten.

The documents we give to new recruits on their first day are as follows:

☐ **Welcome letter.** Welcomes them to their new job, outlines the date their employment begins, and confirms their job title, rate of pay and method of pay. It also confirms the probation period length, and the period of notice required during this time.

☐ **Employee particulars.** We have a form that new recruits are asked to complete in order to provide us with all the particulars we need to keep on file. This includes home address and various contact numbers, bank account and sort code (for monthly wages), national insurance number, and details of their nominated emergency contact.

☐ **Staff handbook.** This goes into detail about the kind of café we are, the ethic of work we expect and the foods we serve. It also outlines our various hygiene, health and safety policies, and various practices we don't tolerate, for example smoking during working hours, and wearing nail varnish.

☐ **Illness notification.** We require new recruits to sign and return this form. It states that they will notify us if they are suffering from a range of illnesses that could contaminate the food that we serve to our customers.

I recommend that you purchase a big lever arch file, and have a section for each member of staff. That way you can be organized, and safely and securely store the data relating to each employee. Examples of our employment documents can be found at the back of the book.

Training

TRAINING FOR YOURSELF

Exactly how much training you will need to undertake before you open your sandwich bar will very much depend on your own personal experience. However, there are certain courses that you should certainly research and invest in.

Food safety

You need to invest in some food hygiene training before opening your sandwich bar. I would recommend you undertake it during or before the the re-fit stage, as much of what you learn will help you decide where to position sinks, the food preparation area, etc. The Chartered Institute of Environmental Health is the most recognized and respected course provider. Visit www.ciehcoursefinder.com to find a course nearest to you.

Café Culture

Our environmental health officer recommended that we each achieve a Level 2 Food Safety certificate before opening, so that's exactly what we did! The course cost £80 each, and we completed it at evening college, one night a week for four weeks. Alternatively we could have taken a one-day course for the same price. The course provided us with a thorough understanding of food safety, storage, preparation, contamination, refrigeration and best methods of working. We need to sit a refresher course every three years.

Barista training

Making a perfect cappuccino or latte is quite a fine art, and if you're investing in a manual machine I would most definitely recommend you undertake some training. This does not have to be expensive, as any coffee machine or coffee bean supplier worth their salt should provide new coffee shop customers with some kind of training. Gaggia, Caffe Society, Coopers – if you search online you'll find details of the kinds of training firms such as these provide.

Café Culture

The supplier we bought our machine and coffee from offered us the use of their demonstration suite prior to our opening. We took full advantage of it, and spent many an afternoon steaming milk and tamping coffee, until we had perfected the art!

Business training

If you're totally new to business then it may be worth contacting your local college and researching any courses they run under the heading 'Business and Finance'. My local college has courses on a range of subjects including bookkeeping, using Excel, and promoting and advertising your business. These courses range from an afternoon to a series of evening classes, and range from £60 to £180.

TRAINING FOR YOUR STAFF

We have developed a simple training manual that each new starter works through. They're not thrown in the deep end, they are trained a stage at a time, learning and becoming confident with new skills before moving on to the next stage. This does take longer, and believe me I totally understand that sometimes time is a luxury you don't have! But we've definitely learnt that time invested now will mean a much better member of staff later on.

Any training programme you develop for your new staff should include the following sections.

Food safety

The law states that it is your responsibility to ensure that your staff are supervised and trained in food hygiene in a way that is appropriate for the work that they do. This basically means that you don't need to send each and every member of staff on an expensive food safety course, but you do need to pass on your own knowledge and explain about the important issues of cross-contamination, cleaning, chilling and cooking.

Why not consider putting helpful notices up around the kitchen to remind staff of critical food safety rules? Perhaps mount a notice on the fridge reminding staff of storage and labelling rules.

Portion control

The earlier you can establish set portion control guidelines for each food that you serve, the earlier you'll have control of your bottom line. This is critical if you want your business to make money. With this in mind you should train your staff how to make each and every item on your menu.

Presentation

Your customers want consistency in the food they buy from you. Each member of staff should therefore be trained to make each item of food in the same way, every time.

Customer service

Decide how you want your customers to be served – what style, and what tone. Think about how you'll introduce new customers to your menu, or how you'll recommend foods to them. Once you have established what you want, train your staff to serve in this way.

Consider providing staff with a handout of suggested phrases, sales techniques and conversations to have with customers. Carry out a training session and use role-play so that you can coach them in the correct way of doing it.

Alarm Bell

Don't be afraid to dictate how your employees serve customers. If you leave it up to each individual member of staff to decide on what they say, how they say it and the service that they give, then you'll end up with a very disjointed sandwich bar and customers will feel confused.

Marketing – creating a big splash launch!

How you market your sandwich bar in the weeks prior to opening, and in its first few months, will have a massive impact on the speed at which you become established, and ultimately start making money. Why? Because it's all very well having a great product, but if you can't find a way to communicate your idea to your target customers you won't be selling very much!

Marketing is all about informing people, and then keeping them informed. In the case of your sandwich bar it's about telling people what you do, what makes you special and why they should try you, and then constantly reminding them, again and again and again. You developed your key messages in Chapter 2. Now's the time to put them to work.

So what are the tools you can use to market your new business, and launch it to the general public?

☐ **Collateral** – In other words, physical items such as menus, menu boards and posters designed to showcase what you do and what makes you special.

☐ **Public Relations** – This would include sending press releases announcing your imminent opening to local press, or perhaps staging a photo shoot with a local celebrity.

☐ **Promotions** – Giveaways, or special offers designed to entice people in.

☐ **Advertising** – This could be in local papers, local radio etc.

Let's look at these in more detail.

COLLATERAL

Sandwich bar menu

A well-designed menu is vital to a sandwich bar. It is your calling card, and a hastily put together, badly designed one will say that you are a second-rate business, and put many people off.

Look over the examples of menus you collected during your research. Which are easy to understand, which have clever and imaginative design features? Can you copy the style of any for your own menu?

You could design your menu yourself using a PC, and then laminate it to ensure it's hard-wearing. However, as with the development of your brand, I would advise against it. Instead, work with the designer who developed your logo, and ask them to design your menu for you. If they're already undertaking work for you, then a price may be negotiated for the extra design work.

To make your menu as long-lasting as possible, consider including price ranges rather than set prices – for example, jacket potatoes from £2.00. Then, if you decide to put prices up you can do so without having to immediately reprint your menu. It's more than likely that you'll have large menu boards in your shop anyway, and this is the ideal place to display more specific prices.

Alarm Bell

Make sure that you ask a friend to proofread any material you are having printed. It's so easy to miss little spelling and grammatical mistakes, and the result is very unprofessional-looking. Just ensure that they'll be brutally honest with you and not just say everything is great!

Menu boards

The menu boards within your sandwich bar will be what most people look at and choose from. For this reason they should be prominent and easy to read. You could have these printed by a sign-writing company, or you could write them up yourself on black or white boards. Either way, you should ensure that the prices can be rubbed out and altered; this will offer you the flexibility to make changes as and when you need to.

Alarm Bell

All descriptions of food or services your sandwich bar provides have to be clear and accurate. These rules are governed by trading standards, and apply to descriptions given verbally, in writing (in a menu or advertisement) or as an illustration (perhaps a photograph used on a menu).

For example, if you are describing your food as 'homemade' then it needs to be. If you say your soup is fresh, then it can't come out of a can. If you include a crab mayo sandwich on your menu, then it must be crab meat, not seafood sticks (then you'd need to call it seafood mayo).

The Trading Standards Central website is particularly useful (www.tradingstandards.gov.uk).

PUBLIC RELATIONS

If you really want to make a splash, then PR is the way to do it. However, only venture down this route if you have something genuinely exciting to say, as otherwise it will be a complete waste of your time. After all, what journalist would be interested in a 'new sandwich bar opens on Monday' story?

Is your sandwich bar bringing new, fashionable food to the area, something that's never been served before? Are you breathing life into a local delicacy that had been in decline? Perhaps you have overcome personal difficulties to open your own business? Maybe you're lucky enough to know a local celebrity who'll make an appearance on your opening day for a press photo shoot. Perhaps the council are making a big deal about local regeneration; if so, the mayor may pay you a visit to congratulate you for going it alone and opening a business in a regeneration area. Maybe you're prepared to organize a 'Sandwich X Factor' competition and get shoppers in the town centre to vote on their favourite?

These are all examples of stories you could create around the opening of your sandwich bar, and by following these simple steps you could achieve a reasonable amount of coverage in your local media.

☐ **Write a clear and concise press release.** This should be produced on a computer and include the vital 'who, what, why, where and when' of your story. If you're unsure of the style you should use, take a look through the local paper and copy the way the news stories are put together. Include a headline, an introductory paragraph with the main details, and then a few more paragraphs with more detailed information. Make sure you include your contact details, and the dates and times when events will be happening.

☐ **Email your press release to local journalists.** These journalists will work for local newspapers and radio stations. You can find their contact details within the publication, or on the publication's website. Many will simply have a 'newsdesk' email address rather than individual journalist emails. Ensure that the subject heading of the email is the headline of your press release.

☐ **Follow up with a phone call**. The next day, telephone the journalists, explain why you think the story is an interesting one for their readers, and suggest they come down to the café for a visit.

☐ **Set up a photo op**. Most local papers will be happier printing a story if it has supporting photography. Get a friend to take some quirky pictures of you at your sandwich bar, perhaps toasting its opening with some champagne! Make sure the name of your sandwich bar is clearly visible in the background. This photography can be emailed alongside the press release.

PR is the cheapest marketing tool available, and is way more effective than advertising. Master this and you'll be mastering the art of 'free' publicity. I worked in public relations for ten years before starting up Taste. However, if you don't have any relevant experience, and you don't feel confident enough to go it alone, you could sign up to a PR course, or consider seeking advice from a consultant, such as the firm my husband and I run (www.sutherlandcomms.com).

PROMOTIONS

Many new stores use a promotion as a tool to get people in the door in the first few weeks of opening. The idea is that the financial incentive is so attractive that target customers simply cannot ignore it, and are tempted in. Your job is then to dazzle them with the amazing food and customer service so that they keep coming back once the promotion is over, and the prices increase to their regular level.

You could consider offering customers a free coffee with every sandwich bought. Coffee is an excellent giveaway as it costs you hardly anything to produce, but the customer's value perception is high. Perhaps develop an introductory meal deal, grouping together likely lunch partners such as sandwiches, crisps and a drink. Maybe use a loss leader (an item on your menu that is under-priced) to tempt people in; you'll soon make the money back on the loss leader when they buy add-on items, or become a regular customer.

Café Culture

In the first few days of opening we asked groups of friends to don branded T-shirts and give out menus and promotional flyers all over the town centre.

Our promotion gave people the chance to 'have a drink on us' and offered customers a free coffee with every sandwich bought. We also created a loss-leading breakfast deal, offering customers toast and tea/coffee, or bacon rolls and tea/coffee at greatly reduced prices.

These promotions were incredibly successful at getting people in the door. Plus, we managed to turn virtually every customer into a regular, and they still shop with us today.

Alarm Bell

Make sure that you include terms and conditions on every promotional offer you market. When will the offer start and end, what does it include and not include, who does it apply to?

ADVERTISING

I'm not going to talk too much about advertising, as I genuinely do not believe that local advertising is a very cost-effective way to market a small business. You're far better to spend time leafleting the local area and creating clever and fun PR stories.

However, if you do decide to advertise through your local paper or radio there are some golden rules you should remember: first, ensure that people in your local area read the publication you choose, and second, have your advert professionally designed. Also, build a coupon, perhaps offering a free drink, into the advert. That way you'll see real results, and actual customers coming in through your door.

Café owner bootcamp

Wow. Take a moment to consider how far you've come and what you've achieved! You're about to open your doors to the great British public and will soon be able to call yourself a café owner!

> **Alarm Bell**
>
> If you've got this far and you have genuinely done all of the research and planning I've suggested in the previous chapters, then you can be confident and positive that your business will be a success. However, if you've skipped sections, and if deep down you know that you've not been as thorough as you could have been, then in my opinion you're walking on very thin ice.

Now comes the part where you transform yourself into a capable and in control café manager . . . Hang on, though. Have you ever served food before? Have you actually stood behind your serve-over counter and made a customer a sandwich? Have you fired up your coffee machine and made a list of drinks to order at double time?

We hadn't! Never ever. That's why we held a family and friends event, a few days before our actual opening day, in order to get the hang of things and iron out any niggling issues.

You may have worked in food retail before, you may have previous bar experience, or perhaps had a job as a waiter in the past. Excellent – this will all serve you well. I would still recommend a dry run day though. After all, you're marketing and promotions could be so successful that you're faced with a queue out of the door on your first day. Will you and your new staff be ready for that?

OPEN DAY

☐ Organize the 'open day' event to take place two or three days before your scheduled first day of trading.

☐ Approach the day as you intend to approach your first day of trading. Set up serve-over counters with the food you'll be serving, have staff positioned where they'll be during a usual day, have menus available.

☐ Invite as wide a selection of family, friends, old colleagues and business acquaintances as you can. We suggest you send the invites out two or three weeks before the event, to ensure as many as possible are available to attend.

☐ Perhaps leave the time of the invite as open as possible. We asked for people to arrive any time between 11am and 2pm, in this way recreating the 'real' lunchtime period when customers call in for lunch at anytime that suits them. It means you'll have some mini busy periods, and some quieter periods, and will get a real feel for a 'normal' day.

☐ Put a prominent sign up on the doors of your sandwich bar, making clear that you're hosting an opening party, and that guests are by invitation only. Otherwise you'll end up serving all the passers-by too.

☐ Try to avoid relaxing, and becoming sidetracked chatting to friends and family. The whole purpose of the day is to test run your sandwich bar, to be sure that you're ready for real customers. Don't waste this opportunity. You can chat and celebrate with champagne later!

☐ Have an agreed closing time, when your practice customers should leave. This then also gives you the opportunity to test out your close and clean procedures.

☐ Once the sandwich bar is shipshape, sit down and consider what you've learnt from the day's trial run.

☐ Did your systems for food ordering and production work, or were customers and staff confused and muddled? Were your staff in control, able to talk to customers about the food they were serving and sticking to the portion controls for sandwich fillings, or do you think they need significantly more training? Did you know how to make all the coffees requested, or do you think you need a bit more practice?

☐ Now take what you've learned and tweak your systems and processes, in preparation for your first day!

ROLLER-COASTER RIDE!

At this point I feel I should pre-warn you a little about what you should expect emotionally and physically from the next few months.

Physically you're going to be working extremely hard. If, like us, you have worked in office-based jobs throughout your career to date, then you're going to be using muscles you didn't even know you had. I certainly suggest some comfortable shoes, because your legs will *ache*, and I mean ache, at the end of every day.

 Find yourself a good osteopath before you open. Any niggling problems with your back or posture will soon turn into painful problems when you begin working on your feet all day.

You'll also need to make sure you find time to eat. This may sound crazy, as you'll be surrounded by food, but you'll be working all the time, with no let up. You should arrive a little earlier than you need to in order to have breakfast, and ensure you sit down for ten minutes after the lunch rush to have a bite yourself.

Emotionally you'll be pretty beat too, as you'll be on a bit of a roller-coaster ride. On the one hand you'll be elated because you have opened your business, and are the proud owner of a shiny new sandwich bar. On the other hand you'll be worried about money, and the learning curve you'll be undertaking will be incredibly mentally taxing: understanding food production and ordering, customer service, delegation, staff management, stock rotation, coming up with new recipes for specials, handling difficult customers. You'll of course become an expert, but the first few months will be hard going.

Look to family and friends for support, make sure you get plenty of sleep, and be as organized as you can.

Open for business!

When I think back now to our first few weeks of trading it all seems a bit of a blur. We'd worked so hard to get the shop fitted out, had developed an appetizing menu and had sent teams of friends out to promote the opening with leaflets and promotions.

Yet, the night before, as Richard and I put the finishing touches to the café, organizing tables and chairs and stocking shelves, we still asked ourselves, can we be certain that anyone will even come in, let alone buy our food? But come in they did, and in their droves. Our first week was fantastic, and we were breaking even from day one.

Thank goodness we were prepared, because new customers need to be impressed; they won't forgive your inexperience if they have a bad experience. So how do you ensure that you are prepared for your first day, and what are the important things you need to remember during your first few weeks?

ORGANIZING YOUR FOOD

As I mentioned earlier in the book, estimating how much stock you'll require and how much food to produce is a difficult task in the early days. What is certain, however, is that customers coming into your new sandwich bar will expect to be able to choose from your entire menu, and won't be happy if you have run out of various mixes, fillings and breads.

Revisit your business plan figures. How many customers do you realistically expect to serve on your first day? Remember, if you've marketed your new business effectively then it is highly likely that there will be a significant amount of interest, and you could actually find yourself very busy during your first few days.

Café Culture

We serve approximately 250 customers daily in our café, and we sell a wide range of sandwich fillings. However, to give you an insight, this is roughly how we'd categorize sales:

☐ *Most bought – chicken, ham, cheese, egg mayo, coronation chicken, tuna mayo, tuna melt*

☐ *Regularly bought – pesto chicken, roast beef, houmous, prawn Marie-Rose*

☐ *Occasionally bought – minted lamb, aromatic duck, salmon, piri piri chicken*

Set aside approximately five hours to prepare and display your produce, ready for opening on your first day. Daily food preparation won't usually take this long, but on this occasion you'll be getting everything ready from scratch! I would recommend that you allocate the afternoon before your opening day to this task. Containerize and clingfilm wrap all your mixes and meats. Then, when you arrive in the café the following morning you simply need to uncover, and you're ready to start serving.

For your first day of opening you should consider making approx 2kg of the mixes you anticipate being your bestsellers, 1kg of the mixes you consider to be reasonably popular and 500g of the mixes you think will be least popular.

Each of your mixes (except those containing high-risk items such as salmon and prawns) will have a life of three days. This means that at the end of day one you can assess what you have left, and use that as the basis for the following day's production. This way you keep a constant eye on how much produce you are carrying. Only prepare what you anticipate you'll need, and thus limit wastage.

Alarm Bell

You may buy in your mixes in handy plastic tubs, but this does not mean that this is the best way to display them! I've been in many sandwich bars that let themselves down because they don't think of transferring mixes into nice serving bowls.

ORGANIZING YOUR STAFF

Just as with food, getting the right level of staff for your first few days, and weeks, is tough. The difficulty is that you don't know how busy you'll be, and so don't know what staffing requirements you'll have.

Over-staffing is preferable to under-staffing at this stage. The loss you'll make from wasted wages is far more desirable than the loss to possible business if a customer's first visit is marred by slow service and a chaotic café.

The key, in the early days, is to try to develop a structured sense of routine as early as possible. Define times of the day for certain tasks, and keep a close eye on when your busy times tend to be. That way, by month two you should have a clearer idea of what staff you'll need at certain times and on certain days of the week, thus be able to reduce any 'wasted' staff wages.

Café Culture

When we first opened our staffing levels were as follows:

- ☐ *7am–11.30am – 2 members of staff, serving breakfast customers and food preparation.*
- ☐ *11.30am–2.30pm – 4 members of staff, serving lunch customers.*
- ☐ *2.30pm–4.30pm – 2 members of staff, serving late lunch customers, café clean down.*

As our business has grown, so has our staffing requirement.

ESTABLISHING ROUTINES

I once knew a café owner who 18 months after opening still had not established routines for the daily running of their café. Food preparation was done sporadically, staff responsibilities were not clearly defined, and the end-of-day cleaning rota was patchy and inconsistent. Staff would clean as they saw fit, not following a set process. Often they would even leave at the end of the day having forgotten to mop the floor, leaving the owner to do it before they themselves left for the day.

The owner was unhappy; they felt exhausted and disorganized. They certainly were not enjoying the better quality of life they'd hoped for. *They were slaves to their business.* I vowed that our café would not be run like that, and I urge you to do the same.

From day one, in fact from day minus one, begin planning structured ways of working.

- ☐ Have clearly defined roles for each member of staff, and set their responsibilities.
- ☐ Section the day into key time periods, and define what tasks are important during each.
- ☐ Have processes for food preparation and ordering.

☐ Develop a daily cleaning schedule, and train staff to follow this schedule in the order you've laid out.

In the early days your processes will change and be amended, but that does not matter. The important thing is to set them in place, and constantly be looking for new ways to achieve greater efficiencies from your staff and your working practices.

THE HIGHS AND THE LOWS

As I mentioned, if you've marketed your business effectively then it is highly likely that your first day, or perhaps even first few weeks, will be fantastic. There'll be a flurry of interest, with the local workers and regular passers-by all keen to visit, and be a little nosy about what your new business offers.

Café Culture

We have set roles for staff members during lunchtime. One member of staff (either myself, Richard, or our assistant manager) is stationed at the till and coffee machine, in charge of the café. Two members of staff are stationed at the serve-over counters, and one member of staff is stationed in the kitchen area.

Each member of staff has clearly defined 'priority' tasks that they should concentrate on during lunchtime. For example, those stationed at the serve-over counters should, first and foremost, take orders from customers. If they find they have a lull in demand then their second priority is to re-stock the counter. If the counter is already fully re-stocked then they should clear and wipe tables.

Likewise, the staff member stationed in the kitchen also has set priorities. First, they should fulfil customer orders for jacket potatoes. If there are no orders, then their next priority is to re-stock the serve-over counters. If the counters are already looking beautiful, their priority is to ensure the dishwasher is stacked and that clean plates, cups and cutlery are available.

Not only does this level of micro-management ensure that the café runs like clockwork, it also helps staff to stay focused, and provide efficient and high-quality service during very busy periods. We simply do not do 'flapping'.

Don't be surprised, though, if a few weeks into trading sales drop slightly. This is quite normal and to be expected. The initial furore is dying down, and you're finding your 'natural' takings figure (the figure you can take through the till without advertising, word of mouth, much effort, etc.). During this time you need to do the following:

☐ Be in your café every single day – live it, breathe it and ensure that you are involved in each and every sale (this is the reason Richard and I still always serve at the till).

☐ Establish a conversation with your customers. Read between the lines, observe what they are and are not buying.

☐ Tweak your menu if you see that something may not be quite right. Draw attention to the cheaper sandwiches if you think customers view you as expensive, highlight the pre-ordering service if you think that customers are waiting too long in a lunchtime queue. Does this create a positive improvement in daily takings?

☐ Watch your staff, and coach them in the right way of serving. Do not allow any bad habits to set in.

☐ Look out for patterns in the increase or decrease of sales. Begin to understand the flow of customers and money into your café and till.

Your aim in these first months should be to observe and listen, to get under the skin of your customer, and really understand the nuts and bolts of your business. From here you'll be able to develop considered plans, to help you move on from your first 'natural' takings figure, and to grow and establish your business.

BANKING AND CASH FLOW

Back in 2006, when we were business owner newcomers, one of the things that attracted us to this industry was the simple principle of cash flow. Why? Because most new businesses fail due to either insufficient, stagnant or halted cash flow. This means that they're not making enough money, are making money but are being paid too slowly, or are not being paid at all.

With the fast food industry, this doesn't (shouldn't) happen. Generally speaking, you'll buy the bread in the morning, sell it at lunchtime, and have the profit in your pocket by the end of the day.

Over time you will establish your own systems of running your business, but the one thing that all successful businesses share is their ability to keep incredibly tight records of everything, and have sufficient profit margins on every single item. Here are some tips to getting cash flow right from the start.

☐ **Differentiate between your own money and the business's money.** The money that sits in the till at the end of each day is not yours. It belongs to the business, and before any of it ends up in your pocket it must first pay rent, suppliers and wages. Don't be tempted to dip in for your own needs; you'll end up in a muddle and your cash flow will become confused.

☐ **Set up accounts.** Setting up accounts with all your suppliers is key. You won't be able to do this straight away, but once you've been using a supplier for three to four months they will be happier to consider it. The usual terms are 30 days; this is great as you can hang on to your cash for longer and utilize it as and when you need to.

Once you're up and running, and have all your suppliers set up on an account, you'll find you need to adeptly manage payment of all the invoices. Try to stagger this throughout the month, so that several huge chunks of money are not leaving your account at the same time. Keep the flow of money smooth and consistent.

Perhaps consider setting staff wage payment for a time in the month when other outgoings are low, again as a way to spread amounts leaving the account and ensure that cash flow is smooth.

☐ **Forecast.** Make sure you know exactly what your outgoings are, and forecast each period to ensure you'll have the funds to pay them. Once you've been trading for six months you'll have a very good idea of your weekly produce bill, wage bill, etc. This means that you'll be able to forecast outgoings, and ensure that the monies are accruing in the account to pay for them all.

☐ **Don't try to do it all yourself!** We talked earlier about employing an accountant. Once you've appointed someone, take time to agree what he or she will and won't help you with. We don't have time to learn about tax rates and the ins and outs of loopholes and PAYE codes. We're busy enough running our business! This means that we leave our accountant (thanks, Julie!) to arrange all that. If you have the time and energy to learn the ropes then that's of course fine, but you must be able to do it properly, as a tax inspector could ruin your business in a heartbeat if you've not been declaring things correctly.

The environmental health officer's first visit

Picture the scene. It's your second month of trading. You're still pretty frazzled, getting to grips with running your business. It's about 9.30am. You're making coffees for a small queue of customers. The café is reasonably busy, with a couple of people sitting down having breakfast while reading the paper. You have a new member of staff in the kitchen making up the day's salad stuffs and sandwich mixes. You know she'll be flat out, because the day before the café was very busy and stocks ran low, making for a hectic prep shift this morning.

The next customer you turn to serve produces an identity badge, and you see the words 'environmental' and 'health'. They explain that they intend to head straight into the kitchen and to take a look around, while you carry on serving your customers.

You think you've trained your staff member to use the right colour chopping board . . . You are confident that you're following the legal hygiene requirements . . .

Regardless, you feel a sense of panic begin to spread throughout your entire body.

UNDERSTANDING THE LAW

Local authorities are responsible for enforcing food hygiene laws. To do this, enforcement officers may visit your premises to inspect them. These officers might come on a routine inspection, or they might visit because of a complaint. They have the right to enter and inspect at any reasonable time and will usually come without telling you first. When they think it necessary officers can take samples of food, inspect your records, write a letter to put right any problems, serve a formal legal notice that sets out things you must not do, and in worst cases even recommend a prosecution.

In the case of your first inspection, an EHO will more than likely want to take a look round your café, in cupboards, fridges, store rooms, etc. They will also want to understand what your food hygiene and health and safety practices are, and see evidence that you are following the law. This means that the scenario above is, in fact, very close to what you can expect to happen, and you need to be prepared for it.

HOW TO PREPARE

First, if you're following good food hygiene and health and safety practices then you don't have anything to worry about. In my experience, EHOs are understanding people. They recognised when someone is taking their responsibility as a sandwich bar owner seriously, and are not on a café witch-hunt. However, they are still legally bound to ensure that you are working within the law, so below are a few of the types of things the EHO will inspect during their visit.

Documented evidence

☐ **Legal regulations** – You should have documented evidence that shows what you do, or do not do, to ensure that the food you serve is safe to eat, and that the processes and systems you use are based on the principles of HACCP. The simplest way to ensure that you have this evidence to hand is to fill in an approved FSA guide, such as *Safer Food, Better Business*. Have this guide available in the shop, as the EHO will want to look through it.

☐ **Shop processes** – Temperature control logs for fridges, a full list of your suppliers, your daily cleaning schedule, your weekly 'deep' clean schedule; all shop processes that you should have written down, and documents that the EHO will want to inspect during their visit.

☐ **Staff training** – The EHO will be pleased to see documented evidence of the staff training that you carry out. This should list all the 'critical' food hygiene areas that staff should know about, including the 4 Cs. You should also ensure that any certificates you have gained from your own food hygiene training are held at the shop.

Practical evidence

☐ **Shop processes** – The EHO will be watching how your staff work, and whether they are following safe food preparation and handling practices. For example, do they all have their hair tied back? Are they using the appropriate chopping board for the task at hand? Is what they are doing putting food at risk of contamination? If you have documented processes in place, train, train and train your staff to ensure that they always follow them.

☐ **Food storage** – Is your fridge organized? Is food sitting out at room temperature? How do you monitor use-by dates? Again, if you've worked hard to develop and document processes, then stick to them. If you say you're going to use labels, then use labels. The one item a member of staff forgets to label could be the one item an inspector makes a note of.

☐ **Café cleanliness** – Do work surfaces look like they are cleaned regularly? Is the fridge already starting to build up dirt in the seals and on handles? Of course your written cleaning schedule will provide documented evidence of your processes, but the EHO will also want to see that these processes are actually carried out.

When the EHO visits for their first inspection it is very easy to panic. However, the key to having a positive inspection is to remain calm, to answer all the inspector's questions honestly and accurately, and to make the documentary evidence available for them to review.

HEALTH AND SAFETY INSPECTION

There is much overlap between the issues of food hygiene and health and safety, and in my experience the same EHO will be responsible for enforcing the law for both. Usually, however, the health and safety inspection and the food hygiene inspection will be carried out on two separate occasions. The first health and safety inspection will usually entail a reasonable amount of time talking about health and safety issues, and the EHO will often bring many useful pamphlets and guides. In addition, they won't put on their scary white coat or be interested in looking in your fridges!

Below is a list of the types of things the EHO will want to see during their health and safety inspection.

☐ Health and Safety at Work risk assessment – The EHO will want to see that you've conducted an assessment of the risks posed to customers visiting your shop, and employees working in your shop. This risk assessment needs to be written down if you employ more than four people.

☐ Employer's liability insurance – The certificate should be displayed in the café (this is a legal requirement).

☐ Fire risk assessment and any related certificates.

☐ Disabled access assessment.

☐ Accident log – Demonstrating that you conform to RIDDOR.

☐ The 'Health and Safety Law: What You Should Know' poster should be displayed for staff to read.

☐ Evidence that one member of staff is first-aid trained – Have the certificate to prove it.

They'll also check that you have adequate (see Chapter 3) clean toilet facilities, that your sandwich bar is a comfortable temperature to work in (at least 13 degrees), and that you have a fully stocked first-aid box.

5
SURVIVING SANDWICH START-UP

AT A GLANCE

In this chapter we'll cover:

- ☐ Teething troubles

- ☐ Watching the bottom line

- ☐ Increasing turnover

- ☐ Looking after your staff and taking care of yourself

- ☐ My parting word…

Teething troubles

We've all witnessed it. A new café opens on the high street. The first few weeks seem to go well – it looks busy, with customers coming and going, the owner behind the counter chatting and revelling in the glory.

Then, things start to begin to slip. The word on the grapevine becomes more negative – standards are not as high as they were, staff can be rude, service is slow. The menu doesn't offer the choice people hoped for. It's confusing and expensive. You hardly ever see the owner any more. Customers start to buy their lunch elsewhere.

The truth is that businesses of any age and at any stage can find themselves in difficulty. However, the first six to 24 months are well documented as being the most traumatic and fragile. In fact, the highest failure rate of any new business is during this period.

Café Culture

 For us, our third birthday was always going to be a milestone. We knew that if we reached this point, our business would have beaten the odds, and would be strong enough to weather the storms of the coming years.

Now that your café is open, the hard work must continue, and you'll need to constantly analyse whether your business is delivering, in every sense of the word. But how will you know whether your business is delivering? Well, the simplest gauge is whether you are making money.

I'm often amazed at how many people think it's 'normal' to make no money in the early days of a new business. Perhaps this is the case when millions and millions of pounds have been invested into a new hotel chain, and debt must first be paid off before any profit can be generated. However, when considering a local sandwich bar or coffee shop, it is wrong to assume that financial loss will precede any financial gain.

In my view, there is no reason why a new sandwich bar or coffee shop should not at least break even by the end of its first month. And if you find that you are still barely making a living, are constantly short of cash and are working ridiculous hours by the end of your first three months, then you need to have a long hard look at your business, because something is not right.

The key is to recognize the warning signs as early as possible. In my experience, café owners often see their business as an extension of their personality, and continue down their original track because of pride. This is human nature. However, you must learn to view your business objectively, and if something is not working out, change it, and fast.

No matter how good your original business plan, many of the teething troubles that arise in the first few months will be unexpected. Let's divide these problems into three manageable categories.

LACK OF PREPARATION

These are problems arising from not preparing well enough before the business was launched (even though your preparation may have seemed good enough at the time). These might include:

☐ The food and drink offerings, or the service your café is providing, does not meet customer needs.

☐ Customer demand is not high enough to make a living.

☐ Your cash flow is slow, and the business is short of capital.

☐ The costing and pricing policy is not right.

☐ Difficulties emerge in relationships with partners, family, suppliers or customers.

Although these problems are common, they can eventually destroy your business, so it is vitally important that they are recognized and dealt with promptly.

INFORMATION AND COMMUNICATION PROBLEMS

All too often problems fester away, while the owner is blissfully unaware of the damage being done to the business. For this reason it's really important that you create simple reporting processes to enable you to monitor the following areas:

☐ Sales performance.

☐ Customer feedback.

☐ Profit margins and cash flow.

☐ Wastage.

'STRATEGIC' PROBLEMS

These are issues that arise because of a lack of long-term planning. It's all too easy, once your café is up and running, to get bogged down in your day-to-day café manager role. But you need to remember that you're running a business too. Yes, it's important for you to serve customers, butter bread and steam milk, but it's also important for you to make sure that you have the time to put long-term plans in place, and develop your business.

Strategic planning does not need to be a formal process. Above all, it is an attitude of mind. When thinking about your business, and planning for the coming six months or year, you should consider the following:

☐ Look for ways to spread the load. You should not depend too much on a single customer group or supplier. If you have all your eggs in one basket then your business is vulnerable.

☐ You should plan how to fund the business's growth in the future. For example, do you need to begin setting aside money to fund the purchase of a van?

☐ You should look for ways to keep in touch with the outside world in order to anticipate problems and spot new opportunities. Could you join the local groups such as the Chamber of Commerce?

Obviously, problems are bound to occur. What is important is that you recognize them early, and investigate to discover the real cause, before you create an antidote.

Much can be learnt from making mistakes. The secret is not to make the same mistake twice. Regularly compare actual performance against the original plan, and stay open to change. It's a fact that quite often a business will find success offering products or services that are different from those set out in the plan at the beginning.

Watching the bottom line

In the case of your sandwich bar, you need to keep a constant watch on the financial outgoings, and ensure that they are managed and under control. These outgoings can be split into two areas: produce costs and staff costs.

PRODUCE COSTS

As I mentioned in earlier chapters, the average rule of thumb for good food retailers is around a 65% mark-up. This means that the price you sell your food and drink at is 65% more than the price it cost you to buy it from the supplier.

You should have kept this figure in mind when you first created your menu, and set your pricing structure. This will hopefully mean that, apart from the odd sandwich that you might have miscalculated, 99% of your menu has been priced correctly and has been providing you with a profitable return since you opened for business.

If is has, then excellent – that's what being in business is all about! Now you need to keep on top of the situation, and ensure that the 65% mark-up figure does not begin to slip. It can, and will, mainly due to increases in the price of produce.

Over the past few years the world food industry has seen huge price increases. As I mentioned earlier in the book, since 2000 the price of wheat has tripled, and in 2007 alone wheat prices rose 52%. And it's not just wheat; all food has increased in price, from fruit and vegetables to milk and chicken. Of course, as producers put up their costs, the large wholesale suppliers must too, until eventually you, the small café owner, feels the squeeze.

You therefore need to keep a constant eye on the bottom line, and monitor price increases like a hawk. If you don't act quickly either to raise your prices or reduce the amounts you are using, for example of sandwich filling, then that magic 65% figure will soon begin to slip to 55%, then 50%, and before you know it you'll be losing more money than you're making and it'll be a hard hill to climb to get back to profitability.

STAFF COSTS

Unbalanced staff costs will also affect your bottom line, and you need to keep a constant check on staffing levels. As your café becomes more established, shift patterns will begin to settle into a norm. This is to be expected, and helps to create an atmosphere of stability among staff. However, don't fall into the habit of simply replicating each week's shift schedule, without considering workload, time of year, time of month and anticipated customer spend.

This is tricky in the beginning, but by month six you should begin to have a clear idea of when the café is busiest, and which days are slower. To help you on your way, here are some tips we've learnt from our café business.

☐ The first week of the month tends to be busy, as people have just been paid.

☐ Tuesday is usually the quietest day of the week, with Monday coming a close second. Wednesday and Friday are always our busiest days, thanks to an outdoor market in the town centre.

☐ The school six-week summer holiday period tends to be slower than usual in our café as many regular customers are taking annual leave. Likewise, before and after a bank holiday tend to be slower than usual.

☐ October, November and December are excellent months for us, as summer diets are long forgotten and customers treat themselves to nice food to help make up for the cold weather and dark mornings.

☐ January and February are the slowest months of the year, as people eat less following Christmas excess, and pay off their credit card bills.

This is reflected in our staff shift patterns. While a Wednesday in November might sometimes require five staff during lunchtime, one in January can often be managed with just three.

Over-staff unnecessarily and you'll feel the impact at the end of the month when wages are paid. Under-staff and you'll feel the financial impact when customers walk past instead of coming in, fearful of the long wait if they join the lengthy queue.

It's quite an art to get staffing right. But it's something you must master.

Increasing turnover

If your business is to be successful, and provide you with the best quality of life possible, then it needs to be generating money during every moment of the day. This means going beyond the basic 'sandwich bar' concept, and considering every possible business opportunity, in order to maximize the output of the space you're renting and the staff you're employing. Here are some concepts you could consider.

OFFER A CATERING SERVICE

There is a huge demand for catered food for office meetings and parties, and if your sandwich bar is situated within a town centre then this is an obvious business expansion route for you.

There are two huge plus points in offering a catering service. The first is that the service is really a natural extension of what you're doing anyway; the second is that it will allow you to maximize the 'dead' mid-morning period and generate revenue when otherwise you'd be twiddling your thumbs.

To do it properly you should consider the following:

☐ **Your menu.** Create a separate catering menu listing the sandwiches, drinks and extras you'll offer. Research other cafés' catering menus; what style do they use, how do they list the options on offer?

☐ **Your service.** Be clear about the level of service you want to offer customers. Do you want to cater for wedding buffets on a Saturday night, or would this be too far beyond the normal working hours of your business? What about a hot breakfast butty spread for an 8am office meeting? Think about how you want this new service to fit into your business, and your life. Don't be scared of saying no.

☐ **Display.** How will you display and serve the catered lunch? A range of platter options is available, ranging from plastic trays and lids through to stainless steel serving platters. What's right for your image and budget?

☐ **Pricing.** The price you charge for your catered lunches should be calculated to reflect the basic price of the produce but also consider production, delivery, display, service (if you're including plates and napkins, etc.).

☐ **Marketing.** Have a poster created and position it in a few prominent places in your shop, and window. Have copies of the menu available in the café for interested customers to take away with them. Perhaps email or write to local businesses, introducing your café and the service. Consider advertising on Yell.com. Form links with other local businesses. For example, if you intend to cater for wedding buffets, perhaps form an alliance with a wedding dress shop and ask them to advertise your service within their brochure.

☐ **Taking orders.** Have a simple ordering system in place, to ensure that customers are dealt with quickly and professionally. I suggest you develop a pro forma order form, with space for all the important and relevant information. We've found it best to encourage customers to place orders via email. That way you can set aside 20 minutes each day to check through incoming orders, and you have the original order in writing in case of any disputes later.

☐ **Payment.** Business customers will expect to be invoiced for the lunch they have ordered rather than pay in cash on the day. Be organized. First check the validity of the business customer before you allow them to have credit from you. We request a copy of the company's letterhead, and then do a quick five-minute search on their website to be sure they are legitimate. Second, prepare a pro forma invoice for each order booked, each with its own individual invoice number. I suggest you do this on the computer on Word, and save electronically. Keep track using a basic Excel spreadsheet of the invoices outstanding, and when payment is due. Make it clear on the invoice what the customer's payment terms are – in the case of most businesses 30 days is expected. Third, keep on top of payments. You need to keep cash flowing, and so as soon as a payment is overdue make contact. If a business repeatedly pays late, and you find yourself spending more and more time chasing payment, you'll need to decide whether the business is worth it. Perhaps reduce their payment terms, or place their account on a 'cash on delivery' status.

Pick the 'low hanging fruit' when it comes to marketing your platter service. The majority of your regular lunchtime customers will work in local offices, and obviously enjoy your food, or they would not be your regular customers! Tell them about your new service and provide them with a menu. This is how we first began to grow our platter business.

OFFERING A PRE-ORDERING SERVICE

If your sandwich bar is constantly busy at lunchtime then you may need to think about ways to serve more people, in the short space of time. One of these ways might be pre-orders. This means that you can be preparing sandwiches late morning, before the lunchtime rush, and then customers can collect them from an 'express till' in the shop. This ultimately helps you to increase the number of sales your café makes, without increasing the size of your premises, or the number of staff you have working through lunch.

To provide a pre-order service you'll need to develop the following:

☐ **Menu**. This could be your usual café menu, or it could be a refined, simpler version accessible on your website, or pinned on local office noticeboards.

☐ **Ordering**. In the past many sandwich bar firms would use a fax back form to enable customer to place orders. This is rather outdated now, and in our experience it's far simpler to use email. Customers can simply email from their desk, and you are able to reply to confirm that their order has been placed. Ensure that you have an ordering cut-off time, and regularly check the order email address to monitor orders being received.

☐ **Production**. You may need to have a member of staff dedicated to producing the pre-orders between, for example, 11 am and 12 noon. Have a set process for orders being produced, labelled and stored.

☐ **Collection**. Clearly signpost what the customer collection process is. If you'd like them to jump the 'made-to-order' queue and head straight to the till then state that on a shop sign. Have the pre-orders stored in an organized way in the nearest fridge.

Alternatively you could deliver the pre-orders to the individuals, meaning they don't have to leave their desk. This is quite a logistical nightmare, though, and would not be financially worthwhile unless your café was receiving multiple orders per day, and a delivery person could carry out a single delivery round encompassing many offices.

PROMOTIONS

Another way to maximize the naturally quieter times of the day is through promotions. Consider a breakfast offer, grouping a hot drink with toast, for a special price. Or perhaps a 'coffee morning' club, offering half-price coffee to those sitting down to a slice of cake between 9am and 11am. Or what about a 'ladies who lunch' promotion, designed to encourage customers into the café on quieter days of the week, such as Monday or Tuesday.

Hot drinks are a fantastic promotional tool, as the cost to you is tiny, but the perceived value to the customers is huge!

Looking after your staff and taking care of yourself

According to accountancy firm Deloitte's study *Entrepreneurship UK 2008*, 31% of small business owners identified a shortage of quality staff as the main barrier they face to achieving business growth. As a small business owner myself I couldn't agree more. It's a simple equation . . .

The right staff and a stable workforce = happy owner and growing business.

The wrong staff and a constantly changing workforce = unhappy owner and floundering business.

You will find that the recruitment and probationary process of a new member of staff is time-consuming and distracting. Your end goal should therefore be to employ a reliable and committed team of staff, who become 'long-timers' and who develop with your business. To achieve this you should focus on the following.

☐ **Motivation.** Once a staff member is successfully through the probationary period, and is trained in the basics, then the key to getting the most out of them, and to them sticking around, is motivation. This comes through coaching, ongoing training and reward.

☐ **Coaching**. We have found the most effective way to coach staff is through regular individual appraisals. For us it works well to do these every six months, but annually would also be fine. We use these 30-minute meetings to understand what motivates the member of staff, and whether they have any goals they'd like to work towards, such as more responsibility or a promotion. We also use it as an opportunity for the member of staff to discuss any issues they may have, and for us to assess their performance. We set a series of targets for the next appraisal and decide on particular training requirements to help the member of staff meet these targets.

❑ **Ongoing training**. We hold group training refresher sessions twice every year, normally on a Sunday when the shop is shut, and including the entire staff. This gives us a chance to revisit portion control, coffee production, food presentation, etc. It also gives us a chance to announce any major changes, or keep staff up to date with plans for the business.

❑ **Reward**. We've introduced some incentives. After all, if you are asking your staff to give 110% every day then you should reward them. For us the right approach is to run a 'spot bonus' scheme. Our staff receive spot bonuses when they excel. We find this works far better than a traditional Christmas bonus, which does not really incentivize staff as they are not singled out for their hard work. We also take our staff on a night out twice a year and the drinks are on us. Alternatively you could consider offering your staff the promise of a staff outing, or introduce an award scheme.

And talking of reward, you can't forget to also look after yourself! It is very easy for the dream of a better life to become the nightmare of business ownership. After all, where do you draw the line between your business life and your personal life? How do you keep a balance, and not become consumed by the running of your café?

The answer is structure. A set structure. You have to make time for your own relaxation, and not let the business consume you.

Keep in mind what your personal goals were when you set out on this life-changing journey. Did you want greater work–life balance, to spend more time with the family, to use this business as a stepping-stone to greater things?

My parting word . . .

Opening our own sandwich and coffee bar has been immensely gratifying, and has eventually led to a flexible work–life balance, and a financially sound income for our family. Yes, the marketplace may be getting tougher, but I believe there's still plenty of opportunity out there for hard-working, enterprising café owners who aren't scared of a little competition.

EXCERPTS AND EXAMPLES

AT A GLANCE

In this chapter we've provided examples and excerpts of the following documents:

☐ **Recruitment example forms**
  – Application form
  – Job specification
  – Employee personal details form
  – Pre-employment medical questionnaire
  – Agreement to report infections contract

☐ **Publicity**
  – Press release

☐ **Staff training and appraisals**
  – Staff handbook excerpts
  – Appraisal form

☐ **Café management example forms**
  – Customer food complaint form
  – Produce order form
  – Delivery check list
  – Weekly temperature checks form
  – Food wastage sheet

Recruitment example forms

APPLICATION FORM

Prospective Employee – Personal Details

Name:_____ Today's date:_____

Age:_____ Date of birth:_____

Address:_____

_____

_____

_____

Contact telephone numbers: _____

Contact email address:_____

Do you smoke? _____

Are you a vegetarian? _____

Do you have a work permit/visa? (if applicable) _____

Any holidays booked? _____

When could you start? _____

Any health problems? _____

How long have you been looking for employment? _____

Do you have any relevant experience? Please give details.

_____

_____

_____

_____

_____

Is there anyone we could contact for an employment reference? Please provide
contact details.

_____

_____

_____

If we think you might be suitable for the position we will contact you in the next few
days and ask you to join us for an interview. If not, then we apologize but we won't be in
touch, we do thank you nonetheless for taking the time to complete this form.

JOB SPECIFICATION

Job Specification

Role	Catering assistant
Reporting to	Shop manager
Hours	Flexible shift based
Rate of pay	18+ £5.60 per hour

A catering assistant at Taste is friendly, efficient and knowledgeable.

The following points show the main day-to-day responsibilities of the role:

☐ Serving customers

☐ Preparation of food for sale, including salad bar ingredients such as potato salad, homemade coleslaw, sandwich mix fillings and preparation of cheese, meats, etc. for sandwich counter.

☐ Preparing to order sandwiches, wraps, baguettes, etc. for customers.

☐ Preparation of pre-packed sandwiches for sale.

☐ Sandwich delivery round.

☐ Preparing to order jacket potatoes and salad bowls for customers.

☐ Preparing to order drinks including coffee, tea, smoothies and milk shakes.

☐ Ensuring the kitchen is kept clean, table-clearing, and produce re-stocking.

☐ Shop close clean down routine.

Full training will be given.

EMPLOYEE PERSONAL DETAILS FORM

Employee – Personal Details

Full name_____

Date of birth_____/_____/_____

Address_____

_____

_____

Start date_____/_____/_____

Contact telephone numbers_____

Do you have a national insurance number?_____*(Please list)*

Bank name_____

Account number_____

Sort code_____/_____/_____

Emergency contact name_____

Emergency contact telephone number_____

Signed_____   Date_____

Once filled in and signed, please return to the Shop Manager along with your P45. (If you have one.)

Without this information, your salary is unable to be paid.

PRE-EMPLOYMENT MEDICAL QUESTIONNAIRE

Pre-employment Medical Questionnaire

Name of employee: ....

Address: ....

....

....

1. Have you ever had or are you known to be a carrier of typhoid or paratyphoid fever?
Yes / No

2. Are you now, or have you over the last seven days suffered from:

☐ Skin rash   Yes / No

☐ Boils   Yes / No

☐ Diarrhoea and/or vomiting   Yes / No

☐ Recurring bowl disorder   Yes / No

☐ Discharge from the eye   Yes / No

☐ Discharge from the ear   Yes / No

☐ Discharge from the nose   Yes / No

☐ Discharge from the gums/mouth   Yes / No

3. Have you travelled abroad in the last three weeks?   Yes /No

4. Have you been in contact with anyone at home or abroad who may have been suffering from typhoid or paratyphoid fever?   Yes / No

---

Details of general practitioner

Name of GP: ....

Address: ....

....

Telephone number : ....

The answers to the above questions are to the best of my knowledge accurate and I acknowledge that failure to disclose information may lead to termination of my employment.

Signed: .... Date: ....

AGREEMENT TO REPORT INFECTIONS CONTRACT

Agreement to Report Infections

Name of employee: ....

Address: ....

....

....

I agree to report the following to my line manager as soon as practicable.

1. Vomiting.
   Diarrhoea.
   Septic skin lesions (boils, infected cuts, etc. – however small).
   Discharge from ear, nose, mouth, eyes, or any other site.

2. After returning and before commencing work following an illness and/or diarrhoea or any of the above conditions.

3. If any member of my household is suffering from diarrhoea and/or vomiting.

4. After returning from a holiday during which an attack of vomiting and/or diarrhoea lasting two or more days has occurred.

Signed: .... Date: ....

Publicity

PRESS RELEASE

10 May 2008

<u>Romford sandwich bar awarded title 'Essex New Company of the Year 2008'</u>

Taste (UK) Ltd, the family-run sandwich, salad and smoothie bar based on Romford's Western Road, has been awarded the title of 'Essex New Company of the Year' at the annual Essex County Wide Business Awards.

Taste, which was opened in May 2006, fought off stiff competition from young businesses across a wide range of industry sectors around the county. These included hairdressers, accountancy firms and training companies. It was awarded the accolade because of what the judging panel considered to be outstanding success in its first two years of trading, and because of the high-quality, fresh handmade food, packed office delivery services and a rapidly expanding party and office meeting catering business.

After being awarded the accolade from the judges, following a gala dinner on 9 May at the Cliff's Pavilion in Southend, Richard Willis, co-owner said, 'We are over the moon. We turned two on 8 May, so what a wonderful birthday present! How fantastic for Romford to be able to boast it has the best new business in the whole of Essex!'

'The award will take pride of place in our café, alongside our 2007 Havering Young Business of the Year Award. We're always talking to our regular customers, and listening to their feedback and comments of support. We just know they'll be happy for us! This award is a massive bonus for us, and I have to say that our staff deserve a huge amount of the credit for all their commitment and hard work.'

ENDS.

About Taste (UK) Ltd

Taste was founded in the spring of 2006 by partners Jill Sutherland and Richard Willis, with the aim of serving food that is healthier than the fast food norm. We were tired of the pre-packaged, boring food choices available to us and wanted breakfast and lunch options that tasted great, were healthier and were also affordable. To achieve this we make our sandwiches and salads freshly by hand each day from naturally wholesome and delicious ingredients. Our soups are 100% natural, and our cakes really are homemade, we don't just say they are! We're not about fads, deprivation or starvation. What we are about is great-tasting food that's good for you.

Our business's scope is three-fold. First, Taste Café provides local workers and shoppers with the option to either sit down or take away our food and drink. Second, Taste to Share is our outside catering service which provides buffet food for office meetings, parties, etc. Third, Taste to You is our lunchtime delivery service, through which we deliver en-masse or individual lunch orders to businesses throughout Havering.

To learn more visit www.tastesfresh.com

Press Contacts

Insert contact details for journalists.

STAFF TRAINING AND APPRAISALS

STAFF HANDBOOK EXCERPTS

Section 1 – What do we expect of you?

It's really important that all of our staff are…

Friendly, efficient and knowledgeable.

<u>Friendly</u>

☐ Why? Because it's important that our customers feel welcome in our café. We know that everyone has a different 'style' of serving customers, and that's OK, but we do ask that once trained, you stick to the 'Taste' way, to ensure standards are kept high. It's all about being helpful, courteous and polite, and smile!

<u>Efficient</u>

☐ Why? Because working efficiently means that you are doing a job in the best (not just fastest) way possible. This means fewer mistakes, better quality and quicker service. Keeping our customers happy!

During service you'll always have a set role; you'll never be 'doing a bit of everything'. This means you can take responsibility for your area, and work as efficiently as possible.

You'll also always be asked to keep talking! This is because we work as a team, and a team is only successful when everyone keeps talking. So communicate which jobs you are working on, how long food orders will take, and what you might need help with.

<u>Knowledgeable</u>

☐ Why? It's important that our customers feel confident that we know our food. Whether that's by being able to explain to a customer what pesto is, remembering their usual sandwich and how they like it, or by explaining the ingredients in one of our 'Designed for You' range. Once trained, you'll be expected to know about the food you are serving, and to talk confidently to customers.

Section 2 – Staying safe

A café can be a very dangerous environment. So it's important that staff understand the dangers, and how to protect themselves and the customers.

First, please make yourself aware of the Health and Safety poster located in the office area of the café. Please also follow the basic procedures we have put in place.

☐ *Knives/slicers*

Sharp knives are stored safely in one of two cutlery drawers. The exact storage location of particular knife types will be explained during your induction. It is vital that all staff follow these instructions so that everyone is able to take care and avoid injury. NEVER submerge knives in the sink in washing up liquid to soak and leave unattended, and NEVER with the blade facing up in the dishwasher.

☐ *Hot cooking*

The electric hob in the kitchen remains hot following its use. Staff should take care to notice whether the red light is on to signal that the hob is still at a high temperature.

The grill used for cooking sausage and bacon is very hot, and only the black parts of the handle should be touched. Grease should be regularly wiped from the grill plates carefully to avoid build up, and fat spitting.

The grill used for toasting sandwiches is very hot. Staff should use the tongs and knife provided to remove toasties, not their hands.

☐ *First aid box*

A fully stocked first aid box is provided for staff use. The manager will show you where it is located in the shop.

☐ *Accident book*

The shop has an accident log. The shift manager should record any staff or customer accident, no matter how minor, within the log. It is the staff member's responsibility to make the shift manager immediately aware of any accident taking place within the café.

☐ *Fire safety*

Taste has a fire safety process, which the shop manager is trained to carry out. This includes a fire alarm, fire blanket and fire extinguishers within the cooking and customer areas of the café, and an evacuation system. Your daily role, to ensure the dangers of fire are limited, are as follows:

– To ensure that customers do not block exits with parked pushchairs, etc., and to notify the manager if this is a concern.

– To ensure that fire extinguishers/blankets are not tampered with (potential for this in customer area, children can play with fire extinguishers), and to notify the manager if this is a concern.

– To inform the manager quickly and calmly if a fire breaks out.

– To follow the manager's instructions regarding fire evacuation process.

Section 3 – Safe food preparation and storage

It is our responsibility to ensure that we always comply with the regulations relating to food preparation and sale. This section is therefore very important, and you must read, and understand it all.

To begin with, to follow is some useful information for you, as a food handler . . .

<u>Food handlers and the law</u>

Everyone who deals with food as part of his or her work has a legal responsibility to safeguard food. Generally speaking your legal responsibility means that you must ensure that:

☐ You keep yourself clean.

☐ You keep your workplace clean.

☐ You wear suitable clean clothing.

☐ You do everything possible to protect food from contamination.

☐ You store, prepare and display food at safe temperatures.

☐ You tell us if you have any symptoms of a food-borne illness (sickness, upset stomach, etc.), or other illness and conditions.

You must also ensure that you do not:

☐ Do anything that would expose food to contamination.

☐ Sell food that is unfit for human consumption.

☐ Work with food if you have food poisoning or similar symptoms until we, or your doctor, say it is safe to do so.

<u>Personal hygiene</u>

It is vital for all staff to follow our personal hygiene guidelines, as this prevents bacteria coming into contact with food, and spreading.

☐ You should be dressed as required by the 'Taste Dress Code' in the Housekeeping section of the handbook.

☐ You should always wash your hands in hot water, using the antibacterial handwash provided, before preparing food.

☐ The right-hand sink in the kitchen is for hand-washing only. Do not wash dishes or any food produce in this sink.

☐ You should always wear gloves when preparing food. And change your gloves each time you begin a new task.

☐ You should not touch your face or hair, chew gum or eat, while preparing food.

☐ You should have removed all jewellery (except wedding band) from your hands. This includes watches, bracelets, etc.

☐ Your hair should be securely tied back.

☐ You should have put on a clean Taste apron.

☐ You should be 'fit for work' and not carrying an illness which could cause a problem with food safety. This includes diarrhoea, vomiting, skin sores, etc. If you feel you may be suffering from such an illness tell the café manager immediately.

Food preparation

It's also vital that all staff follow our food preparation guidelines, as this ensures that no cross-contamination occurs and that food is stored safely.

Here are some key points you must remember . . .

☐ Different tools for different jobs. Undertake one food preparation job at a time, and always have a fresh chopping board, knife, gloves, bowl, etc. This way you won't contaminate one food type with another.

☐ You must always label any food which you prepare, open, decant, slice, wash, etc. Labels are provided; you must simply fill in each section and put on the outside of the tub where it can be seen. If you forget, guidelines to use-by dates are on the fridge and freezer doors, or just ask the manager who'll be happy to remind you.

☐ Always clean and clear as you go. Remove all packaging, plastic, string, etc. This reduces the chances of any debris getting into the food as you prepare it.

❑ Always follow the Taste recipe book instructions. This is because weights, measures, possible allergy issues have all been considered, and by failing to follow the recipe instructions you could put a customer at risk.

❑ Only remove ingredients and foodstuffs from the fridge or freezer when you need to use them. Don't leave things sitting out at room temperature when it's not necessary.

❑ Keep food covered as much as possible, to prevent the possibility of anything falling into it.

❑ If you think anything has contaminated the food tell the manager immediately.

❑ If a customer has a food allergy and queries the ingredients of a dish, don't guess! Ask the manager who can help you.

❑ When you are re-heating food always use the probe provided to ensure it's piping hot! Undercooked food could be very dangerous and make a customer ill!

Section 4 – Cleaning

It's very important for our café to be clean. This is because it makes it not only more hygienic, but also safer.

To follow are some important points for you to remember.

❑ Dirty cloths are the worst offenders for cross-contamination. If you are cleaning a surface use a cloth, then dispose of it, or use a length of blue roll.

❑ Ensure that you take care not to spray disinfectant spray when open food is close by.

❑ We have a set end of day cleaning schedule. We stick to it strictly so that nothing is missed and everything is cleaned properly. Once trained you must follow the schedule, and not change it or amend it without being asked to do so by the manager.

❑ Clean and clear the workstation area as soon as you have finished a task. Don't let dirty tools, chopping boards, etc. back up.

❑ Wash or wipe away any spills as soon as they happen.

❑ Regularly use the spray disinfectant and blue roll to clean work surfaces and fridge handles.

☐ Bins should be emptied regularly, and stored in the rubbish store area to await twice-daily collections. Wash hand, in hot water, using disinfectant soap provided, after empting bins.

Section 5 – Housekeeping and benefits

☐ *Breaks* – Breaks are to be taken by permission of the shift manager, and the allowance, in accordance with the Working Time Directive, is 20 minutes for any shift that is 6 hours or over. Breaks must be taken on the premises unless the shift manager gives permission otherwise.

☐ *Shift schedules* – Staff shifts are confirmed 1 week before commencement. However, flexibility is required in order to cover sick/holiday leave and any additional workload.

☐ *Sickness* – If you cannot work because of illness, you must inform the shop manager no later than 2 hours before your shift is due to commence on the first day and each subsequent day when you are unable to work. It is your responsibility to ensure that you have the Shop Manager's emergency contact details at home, and that you have the means to make contact via telephone conversation. Text message communication is not acceptable, nor is email. We would ask, though, that staff take a mature approach to sick leave, and should you feel an illness developing, we'd prefer you let us know that day so we can pencil in cover, rather than the following morning when we may find it difficult.

☐ *Holiday* – You are entitled to (current entitlement) paid holiday per year, the details of which are in your contract. Holiday requests should be made by filling in a request form and submitting to the shop manager no later than 2 weeks before holiday is due to start. Holidays are granted on a first come first served basis. The holiday year runs from 1 April to 31 March.

☐ *Notice period* – Contracted staff have a 2-week notice period. Staff within their initial probationary have no notice period.

☐ *Smoking* – Staff are not permitted to smoke during work hours, and we do not allow staff to smoke outside the shop during breaks as this is unprofessional and creates a bad image. Any staff that do smoke should ensure that they do not smell of tobacco while they are at work.

☐ *Disciplinary and dismissal procedure* – Please refer to your Statement of Contract of Employment.

☐ *Wages* – Staff wages are paid by electronic transfer (BACS) into the employee's bank account on the 6th of each month.

☐ *Mobile phones* – Staff must have their mobile phones turned off and in their locker during working hours. Staff are permitted to use their mobile phones during break time only.

☐ *Friends and family* – While your friends and family are welcome as customers of the shop you are discouraged from socializing with them while you are working, as this creates a bad impression and has the effect of reducing the quality of service to other customers.

☐ *Personal hygiene and dress code* –

Personal hygiene

☐ You should be clean, freshly washed, and presentable.

☐ Hair should be clean and tied back away from the face. Hair hanging in the face is unacceptable, as is hair tied to hang in front of the body.

☐ No perfume or aftershave with a strong scent.

☐ Jewellery should be kept to a minimum. Rings should be limited to those on your wedding finger. Only one pair of earrings may be worn, and no facial piercing is permitted.

☐ No nail-varnish, or false nails, and make-up should be natural and discreet.

Dress code

☐ Trousers are required to be sensible (jeans, combats, etc.) and plain in colour. Shoes should be flat, and non-slip. White apron, provided by us.

☐ Plain white sensible top (T-shirt, shirt, etc.). Vests are permitted in the summer months, however they must be smart and substantial. No visible underwear.

APPRAISAL FORM

APPRAISAL – JANUARY 2007

Your name		Time with Taste	
Job title		Date of appraisal	

Looking back ...

1. Performance in achieving your personal objectives set last time
(To be completed by both you and your appraiser during your appraisal meeting)

What objectives were set at your previous appraisal, or shortly after you joined?	Outcome □ How do you think you've done in achieving this/these objectives? □ Have you found anything difficult? □ Does the objective need to be carried forward?

2. Taste values
(To be completed by both you and your appraiser during your appraisal meeting)

□ **Friendly**
□ **Efficient**
□ **Knowledgeable**

How have you best demonstrated the three values?	Could you have done anything differently? (Give specific examples)

3. Summary of your performance over the last six months
(Fill in your comments before your meeting)

Your appraiser's comments

▶

4. Summary of training and development activities since last appraisal
(To be completed by you before your meeting)

What training and development activities have you undergone since your last appraisal?

Was it of benefit? What have you done differently as a result? Has it improved your skill sets, performance, etc?

And looking forward …

5. Your role at taste
(To be completed by you before your meeting)

What do you want from your job at Taste? Is there anything you'd like to achieve before your next appraisal? Is there any training or support you think you'll need to achieve this?

6. Your personal objectives
(To be agreed by you and your appraiser at your appraisal meeting)

Objective	How we'll measure success	Timeframe

Signed by appraiser: **Signed by you (appraisee):**

Print name: **Print name:**

Date: **Date:**

Café management example forms

CUSTOMER FOOD COMPLAINT FORM

Customer Food Feedback Form

1. Customer name:

2. Customer telephone number:

3. Customer address:

4. Customer's symptoms (Date and time symptoms first occurred, continuing symptom):

5. Has customer seen doctor? Any tests done / samples taken?

6. Customer's visit to Taste (Date and time, which food was consumed, did anyone else in their party also consume this food?):

7. What else did the customer consume that day?

8. What else did the customer consume the day before?

Dear customer –

Taste takes food safety and hygiene very, very seriously, and so we'll take action to investigate this report immediately. We thank you for letting us know. We'll use whatever information you've given to look into the food served and to test the safety of our practices. We advise that you contact all other possible food/drink establishments you've visited in the last 76 hours and provide them with the same information, so that they too can investigate. Food-borne illnesses are often due to food consumed up to 76 hours previously, and not simply the last food eaten.

If you have any questions, please call (insert manager's contact details).

PRODUCE ORDER FORM

Taste Produce Order Form

Supplier – St Hubert's Fine Foods
Account number – TXXX

Telephone number – 0208 885 2453

Date order placed (Order days – Mon and Thur)

Date delivery expected (Delivery days – Tue and Fri)

Order placed by

Product	Code	Quantity
Houmous	2401	
Sliced topside roast beef joint	1071	
Green & Black's White chocolate	4748	
Green & Black's Milk chocolate	4746	
Green & Black's Maya Gold	4749	
Eat Natural (Mixed Case)	2806	
Orange Juice	2920	
Apple Juice	2925	
Harrogate Still Water	2956	
Harrogate Fizzy Water	2957	
Harrogate Sports Cap Water	2958	
This Water – Cran & Rasp		
This Water – Pomegranate	3462	
This Water – Mango & Passion	3469	
This Water – Lemon & Lime	3461	
Orangina	3467	
Sun Blushed Tomatoes 1.3kg pack	1283	

DELIVERY CHECK LIST

Delivery Check List

Before you sign for a delivery, follow the steps outlined below.

☐ Check the order is correct (double-check against our order sheet).

☐ Check packaging/tubs, etc. are sealed and not damaged or contaminated in any way.

☐ Check use-by dates and ensure they provide a minimum of 10 days' life.

☐ If produce is refrigerated or frozen, check its temperature. Use the electronic probe; push it in among the sealed tubs. Record the temperature on the delivery slip.
  - Refrigerated should be between 0 and 5 degrees.
  - Frozen should be 18 degrees or lower.

If the points are all met, then sign and receive goods.

WEEKLY TEMPERATURE CHECKS FORM

Taste (UK) Ltd Temperature Tracker

TEMPERATURE CHECKS   Week starting

am/pm

Item	Mon	Tues	Wed	Thurs	Fri	Sat
Tall Kitchen Fridge						
Tall Kitchen Freezer						
Tall White Freezer						
Serve-over One						
Serve-over Two						
Grab and Go						

Temperature probe collaboration

FOOD WASTAGE REPORT EXAMPLE

Taste (UK) Ltd Food Wastage Tracker

FOOD WASTAGE

Item	Manager	Date discarded	Weight/Quantity	Reason

HELPFUL LINKS AND CONTACTS

1. General business advice

Business Link (England)
www.businesslink.gov.uk 0845 600 9006

Business Eye (Wales)
www.businesseye.org.uk 0845 796 9798

Business Gateway (Scotland)
www.bgateway.com 0845 609 6611

Invest Northern Ireland
www.investni.com

Small Business Advice Service (England)
www.smallbusinessadvice.org.uk

Scottish Enterprise
www.scottish-enterprise.com 0845 607 8787

Workspace (Northern Ireland)
www.workspace.org.uk 028 7962 8113

2. Business management

HM Revenue & Customs
www.hmrc.gov.uk

New employers' helpline 0845 607 0143
Helpline for newly self-employed people 0845 915 4515

National minimum wage helpline 0845 600 0678

VAT registration 0845 010 9000

Health and Safety Executive
www.hse.gov.uk 0845 345 0055

Equal Opportunities Commission
www.eoc.org.uk 0845 601 5901

Companies House
www.companies-house.gov.uk 0870 333 3636

HCIMA (Hotel & Catering International Management Association)
www.hcima.org.uk 020 8661 4900

British Hospitality Association
www.bha-online.org.uk 0845 880 7744

ACAS – Advisory Conciliation & Arbitration Service
www.acas.org.uk

BFA – British Franchise Association
www.thebfa.org

Institute of Chartered Accountants
www.icaew.co.uk

The Law Society
www.thelawsociety.org.uk

Business consultants and mentors – Sutherland Communications
www.sutherlandcomms.com

3. Catering industry

Food Standards Agency
www.eatwell.gov.uk
www.food.gov.uk
www.salt.gov.uk

British Sandwich Association
www.sandwich.org.uk

Health and safety training courses
www.hshtc.co.uk

4. Retail units and business for sale

www.shopproperty.co.uk
www.businessesforsale.com

INDEX